Ballerina

The Art of Women in Classical Ballet

Ballerina

The Art of Women in Classical Ballet

Mary Clarke & Clement Crisp

BBC BOOKS

We dedicate this book to Natalia Makarova
with gratitude

Published by BBC Books
A division of BBC Enterprises Ltd
Woodlands, 80 Wood Lane, London W12 0TT

First published 1987

© Mary Clarke and Clement Crisp 1987

ISBN 0 563 20436 2

Typeset in 12/15 pt Bembo, printed and bound in Great Britain by
Butler and Tanner Ltd, Frome, Somerset

Contents

We would like to express our thanks to Parmenia Migel Ekstrom of New York for so kindly lending us the illustration of Madeleine Guimard visiting the sick, a photograph from a print in her magnificent collection and reproduced in her delightful book *The Ballerinas*. We must also thank Dr Erik Ashengreen for finding for us some rare photographs of the Royal Danish Ballet in the Royal Theatre Collection in Copenhagen.

We owe a great debt to Susan Kennedy, our editor, who scrupulously prepared our manuscript, to Sarah Wergan who not only found illustrations we asked for but produced some beautiful and unfamiliar material as well, and to Ann Thompson who was responsible for the book's very attractive design.

Mary Clarke, Clement Crisp

Introduction

The word 'ballerina' is widely misused and misunderstood. The ballerina is the figure who is traditionally the pinnacle of the ballet – that is, dance in its most refined and élitist form. Yet any girl who wears *pointe* shoes and hits a headline seems automatically to be described as a 'ballerina' – a grotesque misuse of the term. To become a ballerina requires a God-given gift, as well as unceasing hard work and a company to provide a framework which will show off the great artist. The entire apparatus of a major classical ballet company is necessary if a ballerina is to be seen in her proper setting. Certain fine dancers in different disciplines – Isadora Duncan and La Argentina are supreme examples – have dominated the stage in solo recitals, but the ballerina in her true sense is the apex of a pyramid formed by the traditional ballet company and the traditional repertory.

'The era of the ballerina is over,' Dame Margot Fonteyn observed at the close of her television series *The Magic of Dance*, and we ended our previous book *Dancer*, related to Peter Schaufuss's television series about male dancing, with this quote. The new series to which this book is linked, presented by Natalia Makarova, shows that even if the male dancer has now taken the centre of the stage, he shares it with the ballerina in a kind of companionship undreamed of before. Yet the ballerina must ever be the central and proper focus for much of the traditional repertory – ballets such as *Swan Lake*, *Giselle* and *The Sleeping Beauty* which entrance audiences worldwide. It is these works which still offer some of the greatest challenges to the female dancer, and it is their demands, so often unmet in the ballet theatre today, which indicate how rare it is to find a ballerina. However, if the ballerina seems an endangered species, the fault lies not with the increasing importance of male dancing and male training, or changes in attitude, but with the failure of many companies and their schools to capitalise upon women's talents and to create performers capable of filling out the traditional roles with the radiant artistry that ballerinas have shown in the past.

In this book we hope to show the historical process that created the idea of the ballerina, and also something of the rich variety of artistic expression which is implicit in that word. Starting with the first female soloists who won the title ballerina, we demonstrate how the great ballerinas, from Taglioni and Pavlova down to such celebrated artists of our time as Ulanova, Markova, Fonteyn and Makarova, reached the pinnacle of their art and enhanced the artistic life of the world.

In the pages that follow it would be impossible to make an historical survey which

included every significant ballerina: the result would resemble a laundry list. We have, therefore, chosen the dancers whose lives and art we believe cast some significant light upon the identity of the ballerina at any given time. Thus a dancer may be included because she was an eminent figure in the development of ballet, like Marie Taglioni, or she may have been more representative of the life of a ballerina in the society of her time, like Madeleine Guimard. She may have been a great apostle of the dance, like Pavlova or Markova, or she may embody the artistic ideals of a company, like Ulanova or Fonteyn. Our selection will perhaps seem arbitrary, and we are bound to have omitted artists whom various societies and nations will regard as very important, but we have sought to give as broad a view as possible. We would recommend our readers not only to pursue further reading about the great names of the past but also to keep an alert eye on the young aspirant ballerinas of the future.

Every ballerina in a sense sums up both the dance of her time and everything that has gone before. She reinterprets the past for us, illuminates the present, and leads into the future. As the great Danish choreographer August Bournonville said, in the middle of the nineteenth century, 'Every dancer ought to regard his painstaking art as a link in the chain of beauty, a necessary decoration for the stage which, in turn, is an important factor in the spiritual development of the nation.'

Because Natalia Makarova, as programme presenter, is the sustaining link in the television series *Ballerina,* we have thought it proper to begin our story with a portrait of her as a great theatrical performer of our time, before looking back to the long line of dancers who are her ancestors and even daring to look forward to some young dancers who may one day be her heirs.

Natalia Bessmertnova in Les Sylphides.

Natalia Makarova

Natalia Makarova speaks and dances as a ballerina who has bridged two worlds: that of Soviet ballet, with its idealism about dancing and with those enriching traditions which Makarova knew as a product of the Kirov School and company in Leningrad; and that of Western ballet, which she discovered when she chose to remain in the West and work with major ensembles from 1970 onward. In her art she has managed to reconcile these two worlds, although she remains essentially Russian none the less. We can but observe that the effect of Russian temperament and training upon the Western repertory, as seen in Makarova's performances, is magical.

The art of a great dancer, so far removed from that of a good dancer, is mysterious in that it transcends accepted performance manner, breaking the rules and passing beyond the norm. It may be the matter of a superlative physical instrument, such as Alicia Markova's exquisite fragility; it may be the concentration of the spirit in a role, as in Ulanova's Juliet running to Friar Laurence in a surge of impassioned energy. In the first and vital instance it depends upon schooling, on the good teacher inculcating attitudes to movement that sustain the dancer ever after. As with the Jesuits' supposed hold over a man if he has been theirs as a child, so it is with the teacher's lasting influence over the dancer. A great interpretative talent will help us to understand, not through any false reverence or dutiful affection for the past, but honestly and vividly, the continuing theatrical relevance of certain masterpieces. Many ballet companies try to show *Swan Lake* or *Giselle* or *The Sleeping Beauty* as major works of art, but an inescapable fact of the nineteenth-century repertory, as preserved and honoured in Russia, is that its ballets are vehicles whose motor is the ballerina, and any presentation of them is flawed unless its focus is a prima ballerina, mistress of her calling.

One of the sadder aspects of ballet in the West today is that the *assoluta,* able to sail in grandeur through this repertory, is very, very rare indeed. There are many gifted dancers who are technically able and charming. In the classics they are decent performers, 'house' ballerinas in major companies, going through the motions of the old repertory with extreme competence. But that essential illumination shed by great interpreters is rarely present. It is different in Russia, where each generation of dancers seems to produce talent which is richly endowed, richly prepared and able to renew the life force of the old repertory. It is a time-honoured system. In her autobiography *Theatre Street*, Tamara Karsavina, the first great ballerina of modern ballet, spoke of studying *Le Corsaire* with the ballerina Evgenia Sokolova who had earlier shone in that ballet. The great Soviet dancer Galina Ulanova coached Yekaterina Maximova for her first Giselle. The Royal Ballet's Nadia Nerina, invited to appear with the Bolshoi Ballet, was able to study an unfamiliar text of *Swan Lake* with the illustrious Soviet ballerina Marina Semyonova. Armed with the accumulated and priceless knowledge handed down by former interpreters, the débutante Giselle or Odette becomes a vastly better artist, part of a chain of interpretation that may reach back to the very creation of the role she is to dance.

Makarova was born in Leningrad and entered the Vaganova School (which prepares students for the Kirov Ballet and is named after the great teacher Agrippina Vaganova, 1879–1951) somewhat late for a girl, at the age of thirteen, as one of a group of gifted experimental students who were given a concentrated six-year course rather than the normal nine-year training. Her teachers in the school and her coaches in the Kirov Ballet (Natalia Dudinskaya, Alla Shelest and Tatiana Vecheslova) were Vaganova pupils themselves and leading exponents of the classic repertory. Makarova's gifts were clear from the very first, and in her graduation performance of the adagio from the second act of *Giselle* her affinity with the Romantic style was clear. She danced her first Giselle in 1959 at the age of nineteen, during her first season with the Kirov Ballet, and she was subsequently to dance all the classic repertory with the Kirov as well as many of the ballets of the contemporary repertory.

It was in 1970, during the Kirov Ballet's season in London at the Royal Festival Hall, that Makarova opted to remain in the West, seeking there greater opportunities and challenges for her art. (As with Nureyev and Baryshnikov, who also chose to

Makarova and Anthony Dowell in the second act of Giselle *with the Royal Ballet at Covent Garden in 1980.* Previous page *Natalia Makarova and Mikhail Baryshnikov in the bedroom scene from Petit's* Carmen.

live in the West, her decision should in no way be considered political. It was the quest of a fine artist for fresh fields.) Since making that decision, Makarova has confirmed the power of her talent both in the traditional ballerina repertory of the nineteenth century, giving what must be considered definitive performances for our time in *Giselle* and *Swan Lake,* and also shining in such modern full-length works as MacMillan's *Romeo and Juliet* and *Manon,* John Cranko's *Onegin,* Frederick Ashton's *Cinderella,* and Roland Petit's *Notre-Dame de Paris* and *The Blue Angel.* These suggest something of her range and the intensity of her communicative power. She has assumed most of the leading roles in the repertory of American Ballet Theatre, the company which became her home in America, and has also danced in several important modern works with the Royal Ballet.

Tradition is central to the ballerina's art. From her legacy she moves forward to explore her own performing gifts, always remaining conscious of certain laws of stylistic expression. Thus, for example, Makarova's Giselle, her Odette-Odile in *Swan Lake,* Nikiya in *La Bayadère* and Aurora in *The Sleeping Beauty* were an extension of the achievements of her great predecessors, from her teachers Dudinskaya and Vecheslova, through Pavlova and Spessivtseva, to Vazem and leading artists of the nineteenth century: the history of the Imperial Russian Ballet in St Petersburg was implicit in her performances.

Thus it was that in *Giselle* Makarova's performance over a period of twenty years was a process of purification as the role became ever more refined in its expression and more intense in its feeling. Her peasant girl in the first act seemed to have some comprehension of her destiny, knowing that she was to move towards a pre-ordained fate. The Wili, emerging from the husk of the dead Giselle, was a spiritualised extension of her character, and in the two acts the two Giselles were made one. The transparent wraith who rose from her grave at Myrtha's command – how eagerly she danced with the weight of the earth and of human sorrow removed from her! – was no more than animate mist, sustained by the realisation that she is more truly Giselle than ever before. All decoration had been removed from the dance and the performance was pure, true in feeling as in step. Hovering over the kneeling Albrecht, Makarova seemed to lean on the night wind for support. The dramatic tension of the first act was still present in the second act; the intensity of Giselle's madness had its mirror in the exquisite power of the Wili's concern for Albrecht. The terrors of the mad scene, with distraught hands clawing at the air, had a counterpart in the intense spirituality of the ghost, whose every leap was a sigh and whose poses spoke only of compassion.

As Odette, Makarova showed the Swan Queen's grief coming from the depths of her spirit. She was haunted by her swan nature. A recurrent image of flight showed her body aspiring upwards in a flawless arabesque, posed for an eternal second on Siegfried's crossbow as if on an in-drawn breath before taking to the air. Very extraordinary was the effect Makarova achieved on one occasion in the *pas de deux* of the second act by averting her eyes. Her Siegfried (David Wall) looked wonderingly at her. Time and again Makarova turned her gaze away, unable to accept the hope implicit in his presence. Then suddenly she returned his gaze fully and intensely, as if seeking courage in him. Always in her performance, the inner choreographic life of the role was displayed through unhurried spans of movement that started with a seemingly gentle momentum and then gained in wave-like power, curving to a climax, breaking and transferring energy to the next phrase. Odette's leave-taking was no less extraordinary. The swan motif sounded; Makarova turned her head away as if hearing the call of fate that would separate her from hope. She made a final agonised gesture to Siegfried and her arms seemed to change before our eyes, undulating and beating as the personality of the dance itself changed. Human emotion and human form were lost as Von Rothbart's spell took effect and the swan's identity returned with the morning. As Odile, she became a luscious vampiric beauty, her body poised to strike at Siegfried. This was an irresistible Odile, her eyes hypnotising

Natalia Makarova rehearsing the adagio in the second act of Manon. *She is supported by Julian Hosking of the Royal Ballet.*

Siegfried, a malignant vision of the beloved for ever beyond Siegfried's grasp. There was no shallowness about the bravura of the dance, but a heartless and blinding brilliance – the flash of diamonds rather than the glitter of paste.

In such modern roles as MacMillan's Juliet and Manon, or Cranko's Tatiana, Makarova has a wonderful impetuosity. Her Juliet seems to race towards her destiny on a single passionate impulse. Her Manon is a triumph of physical and emotional caprice that fills out the character. It is dancing of exceptional femininity, deliciously and pungently sensual in the first two acts. If Manon is not irresistible, she is nothing, and this Makarova understands. She shows us that Manon's awakening awareness of her sexual attraction and of the rewards it can bring is the key to her personality. The girl who steps from the coach in the first scene may be innocent, but we already sense a kittenish desire to please. The acceptance of Des Grieux's love is a desire for love itself; the decision to take G.M. as a protector is an eagerness for the wealth Manon has admired among the whores at the inn. When G.M. buys her (no difficult task), Makarova shows Manon's hands feeling the necklace he has just given her, seeking and finding in it reassurance for her desertion of Des Grieux. And, when she leaves the lodgings, how magical the quick regretful glance back towards the bed she has shared with Des Grieux.

As a triumphant cocotte in the second act Makarova suggests Manon's veneer of sophistication. But throughout the party scene there is a constant awareness of Des Grieux's presence which haunts every glittering moment. When at last Manon acknowledges her love for him, it is an action as ardent and unthinkingly immediate as any she has made, as, too, is her suggestion of a fortune to be gained from cheating at cards. Drained by suffering in the third act, Makarova makes Manon little more than a ghost. The final duet with Des Grieux is danced with a hectic and swiftly expended energy that is the final delirious effort of Manon's body and spirit.

In what we can best describe as the psychic vitality of Makarova's performances, we are in effect seeing Makarova listening to, in her own words, 'the voice of her body'. It is a voice of great natural distinction and beauty; one that has been superlatively trained and is incapable of a dull or vulgar sound. If Makarova's actions burn with immediacy, the choreography seeming newly minted as she dances, the controls of her Kirov training are ever present. There comes a magical fusion between the body which knows and the dramatic temperament which responds so vividly to the surroundings of performance, to partner, music and audience. Makarova on stage is both intensely outgoing and intensely receptive to the feeling of the moment. She seems priestess of both Apollo and of Dionysos, but her first allegiance is to the discipline of Apollo. The inner life of the dance, which we have sensed in her every performance, often passionate, ever questioning, can speak to us only through the harmonious nobility of the classic manner. It is thus that we hear the essential, the spiritual voice of a great dancer.

The First Ballerinas

Because the origins of ballet as a theatrical entertainment are to be found in the court spectacles of the sixteenth and seventeenth centuries, the first female performers were often the greatest ladies in the land. In 1573 the *Ballet des Polonais* (the Polish Ballet), one of the earliest court 'ballets' in France, took place in the Palace of the Tuileries in Paris. It was, like so many of the court spectacles of that period, making a political statement in that it was intended to suggest to the ambassadors from Poland, lately arrived in Paris to elect Henri of Anjou as King of Poland, that the French monarchy and state would provide necessary support for the alliance initiated by this election and treaty.

Henri of Anjou was the third son of Catherine de Medici, Queen Mother of France, and it was her Italianate tastes, gained from her Florentine upbringing, which had given such impetus to these court displays in France. Now, in this magnificent spectacle, sixteen of her ladies-in-waiting performed in dances that were the culmination of a sequence of songs. Each representing a province of France, they declaimed verses while descending from an artificial, silver-gilt rock to tread through the steps of a 'ballet' whose solemn measures were supposed to indicate laws of harmony and heavenly peace. Finally, each of the ladies presented to King Charles IX of France, Henri's brother, and the Polish ambassadors, gilt emblems which bore symbols representing the produce of their various regions. There followed a general court dance, and it is interesting to note that the performers and the spectators were of the same social order and that dancing, so vital a courtly activity, was seen here as a proper expression of the most important matters of national policy.

Eight years later Queen Catherine de Medici was the inspiration behind the most famous of the court ballets of the period, the *Ballet Comique de la Reine Louise*. This five-hour entertainment, combining song, music, dance, declamation and stage machinery, was the grandest of court ballets. It had of course a political purpose, as it was part of the celebrations staged to mark the marriage of Margaret of Lorraine, sister of Queen Louise of France, wife of Henri III, to the Duc de Joyeuse. During the course of the performance a variety of floats and mechanical devices were used and it is for our purposes sufficient to note that Queen Louise herself, as well as the Princess of Lorraine and several of the ladies of the court, appeared in a miraculous fountain as naiads. Their presence again stresses the fact that dancing was a noble art and one which – even for women – involved the participation of the greatest in the land. It is no exaggeration to view these dancers as the first 'ballerinas' in that they were required to display elegance and skill above the common run of court ladies.

By the beginning of the next century the court ballets of the Valois had given way to less elaborate 'masquerades' in which the female roles were more usually taken by men. Nevertheless, certain noble ladies, including Anne of Austria, the wife of Louis XIII, made occasional appearances in court dances. Their participation was marked by delicacy and noble grace; attempts at any sort of virtuosity or a broader style were left to the men who took the women's parts.

The example they set of dignity and decorum was persistent. Court dancing was governed by stringent rules of conduct and stylistic elegance, and it was these qualities which would mark the performances given by the first professional female dancers seen in France in 1681. By this time court ballet was on the wane and court entertainment in the latter years of Louis XIV's reign had become the province of the professional dancer. It was in *Le Triomphe de l'Amour*, an opera-ballet given in 1681, that the first four professional female dancers – the first real ballerinas – trod the stage. Of these first female stars we know very little, beyond their names. They were Mlles Roland, Le Peintre, Fernon and La Fontaine, the latter of whom, as the leader, was inevitably known as the Queen of the Dance. She did not enjoy this title for long because in 1690 she gave up the stage and retired to a convent in which she spent the remaining four decades of her life.

The position of the female dancer was of course vastly inferior to that of the man. Women were restricted by social convention from participating fully in the opera-ballets of the period; furthermore, the voluminousness of female clothing allowed limited movement. Nevertheless, female dancers continued to appear and excite public attention; Mlle La Fontaine's successor, Marie-Thérèse de Subligny, won a considerable public following, although on technical grounds she was criticized for not being very well 'turned out' at foot and ankle. The question of technical training for the female dancer, as for the male, was to receive significant impetus with the establishment of a proper school at the Paris Opéra in 1713, and by this time Mlle Subligny's successor, Françoise Prévost (1680–1741), had set about establishing the idea of 'the ballerina' both as virtuoso and expressive artist. Prévost was, for her time, an exceptional performer, displaying stronger technique than her predecessors and also, as we surmise, making first steps towards that expressivity which was to be so important a demand upon ballerinas later in the century.

In 1714 Prévost and the male dancer Ballon took part in an entertainment given by the Duchesse du Maine at her château of Sceaux. Part of the fourth act of Corneille's play *Les Horaces* was mimed by the two dancers, an early indication of the quest for narrative meaning in the hitherto formal world of the eighteenth-century dance, but it is Prévost's pupils, Camargo and Sallé, to whom we must turn for the clearest evidence of the emergence of a theme that recurs throughout the history of the ballerina in succeeding centuries – the rival claims of technique and expression.

Marie-Anne de Cupis de Camargo was born in Brussels in 1710. Her grandmother was Spanish and her father had claims to gentility but his circumstances were such

Right *Jean Raoux' celebrated portrait of Françoise Prévost shows her as a bacchante. The painting is more a tribute to Prévost's charms than an actual representation of her appearance on stage.*

Below *Marie Camargo. This engraving, after the painting by Lancret, depicts the ballerina in the shortened skirts she introduced to show off her quicksilver feet.*

Previous page *Mlle de Subligny dancing at the Paris Opéra, from an engraving of around 1700. She is dressed in the height of fashion and is an essentially aristocratic figure.*

that he had to give lessons in the reasonably polite arts of dancing and music. The young Marie-Anne learned dancing as a child and gained sufficient reputation as a prodigy to be taken to Paris for classes with Mlle Prévost. Three months later she made her début in Brussels and then appeared in Rouen, where her father was playing in the theatre orchestra. Even in these early performances her spritely manner and her beauty found great favour with the public, but her career suffered a hiatus when the manager of the Rouen Theatre became bankrupt. However, her fame was already such that the director of the Paris Opéra invited her to appear there. Under her new stage name of Mlle de Camargo (her grandmother's name), she made her début in 1726 in the ballet *Les Caractères de la Danse* (a piece in which her teacher Mlle Prévost had had a huge success ten years before). Critics applauded Camargo's 'liveliness and intelligence', her brilliance and 'airiness' as a dancer. Within two years she had so won Paris's heart that fashions in dresses, shoes and *coiffures* were named after her. Mlle Prévost, by now nearing the end of her career, tried to hold back her young rival by relegating her to the *corps de ballet,* but fate and Camargo's wit saved the situation. At one performance the *danseur* Dumoulin was supposed to appear in a demon's dance but failed to make his entrance. Camargo, seizing her opportunity, took centre stage and improvised. Prévost, by way of marking her displeasure, refused to give Camargo any further lessons and tried to prevent her from appearing in an entertainment at court. The distressed Camargo turned to one of the great male stars of the period, Blondi, who consoled her, offered to teach her and composed a solo for her to dance at court. The enchanting young Camargo benefited from this help and her career as a darling of the public was thus fully launched.

What seized the public's affection? Undoubtedly, for her period, Camargo was technically brilliant, with well-turned-out legs and feet (unlike Prévost) – or so her obituary notice claimed. The Italian amorist Casanova, who saw her dancing in Paris in the ballet *Les Fêtes Vénitiennes*, described her 'bounding like a fury, cutting *entrechats* to right and left and in all directions, but scarcely rising above the ground, yet she was received with fervent applause'. Voltaire wrote that she was the first woman 'to dance like a man' and referred to her as 'the lively Camargo, light and strong in her suppleness'. Jean-Georges Noverre, the great eighteenth-century ballet master, said that she was 'vivacious, light, and full of gaiety and sparkle ... she only danced to lively music, and such quick movements do not permit of the display of grace; but for this she substituted ease, speed and gaiety.'

Plainly, Camargo dazzled people by her charm and the sparkle of her manner, and not surprisingly she sought an excuse to display her twinkling feet: it is recorded that she used to cross the front of the stage close by the footlights from right to left, and then from left to right, performing the *pas de menuet* which the public delighted to watch. She shortened her skirts nearly to the lower calf, as we can see in Lancret's delightful portrait, for this allowed her feet to be seen and also, perhaps even more significantly, allowed her greater freedom of execution.

Male command of the ballet stage in the eighteenth century had much to do with the sheer freedom of movement which men's clothes allowed. Female dancers were still burdened with skirts, panniers and wigs, and it was not until the reforms in dress introduced by the French Revolution and the Empire at the turn of the nineteenth century that the ballerina could seek a technical identity as strong as that of the man. The shortening of the bell-like Romantic tarlatan to the abbreviated skirt, the tutu, that became the uniform dress for the ballerina, stresses the liberation of the ballerina and the birth of her technical domination of the stage.

Camargo was still dancing in heeled shoes, although it has been suggested that she did use a heel-less slipper, even if no evidence exists to prove the fact. Nor is there evidence, beyond rumour, that Camargo, in shortening her skirts and taking, albeit ever so slightly, to the air, also instituted the use of bloomers – the *caleçon de précaution* which prevented any immodesty occurring in the taking of beaten steps or little jumps of elevation.

For a ballerina so famous for her vivacity, Camargo looks serious in the beautiful pastel portrait made of her by Maurice Quentin de La Tour; in contrast to her dance character, her off-stage personality was grave. She was, however, irresistible to men and had many important and influential lovers. One of these, the Comte de Clermont, who was of royal blood, insisted that she leave the stage during the time he was her official 'protector', as he would not share her charms with the public; therefore, from 1735, Camargo quit the Opéra stage. In December 1741 she returned in *Les Fêtes Grecques et Romaines,* and assumed once again all her former popularity. Ten years later she retired to live in quiet comfort, surrounded by six parrots, many other birds, her dogs and one long-lasting admirer. In April 1770 she died, leaving a fine library, a well-stocked wine cellar, a sizeable fortune and an imperishable reputation as the first female virtuoso ballerina.

Camargo's rival, Marie Sallé, represents the other side of the balletic coin – the ballerina as actress. She was born in Paris in 1707, in a family active in the popular theatre of the time. By 1716 she had made her first appearance in London, in the company of her younger brother, as a member of a troupe brought by her uncle, Francisque Moylin, to perform at Lincoln's Inn Fields Theatre. In Paris she appeared in the comic operas which were given at the annual fairs, and she was thought promising enough as a dancer to be given lessons by Françoise Prévost. In 1721 Prévost was indisposed and unable to appear at the Opéra in *Les Fêtes Vénitiennes* and, so as not to disappoint her audience, she presented in her place this young student, who immediately won the public's heart.

In 1726 Sallé danced in the ballet *Les Caractères de la Danse* which was concerned with showing the various emotions, grave and gay, that dancing might evoke. Accounts of this give a first hint of Sallé's claim on our attention, in that the piece called upon dramatic expressivity as well as technical facility. In the following year Sallé was engaged to appear at the Paris Opéra – still dominated by Françoise Prévost as its leading ballerina – and at this time there began that rivalry in the public mind between the dazzling Camargo and the graceful and emotionally communicative

Sallé. A contemporary poem, written by Voltaire and first published in the *Mercure de France* in 1732, captures exactly the rival claims of these two ballerinas:

> *Ah! Camargo, que vous êtes brillante*
> *Mais que Sallé, grands dieux, est ravissante!*
> *Que vos pas sont légers et que les siens sont doux!*
> *Elle est inimitable et vous êtes nouvelle:*
> *Les Nymphes sautent comme vous,*
> *Mais les Graces dansent comme elle.*
>
> (*Ah, Camargo, how brilliant you are*
> *But, dear heavens, how ravishing is Sallé!*
> *How light are your steps and how gentle are hers!*
> *She is inimitable, and you are new:*
> *The Nymphs leap as you do*
> *But the Graces dance like her.*)

Camargo represented the public appeal of the virtuoso, an attraction that the public still knows today. Sallé, by contrast, was part of that movement towards greater meaning in dance that stretched from the dramatic productions of the English choreographer John Weaver in the early years of the eighteenth century, and the mime performances at Sceaux in which Françoise Prévost and Ballon had participated, to the work of later choreographers such as Hilverding and Angolini. It reached its height in the work of Jean-Georges Noverre, and was given its best-known expression in his book *Lettres sur la Danse et les Ballets* (which contains, *en passant,* illuminating comments on several of the great dancers of the period, including the one already quoted on Camargo).

Sallé's years in Paris were broken by journeys to London, which can be understood as a quest for new audiences as well as for financial reward, and also, perhaps, for greater artistic freedom than she could find in the stifling world of the Paris Opéra. In 1733, on one of these London visits, Sallé staged the ballet pantomime *Pygmalion,* which created a furore. The *Mercure de France* provided a lengthy description which suggests how Sallé retold the story of the sculptor whose great statue of a woman is brought to life. The account concludes: 'You can imagine, Sir, what the different stages of such an action can become when mimed and danced with the refined and delicate grace of Mlle Sallé. She has dared to appear in this *entrée* without pannier, skirt, or bodice, and with her hair down: she did not wear a single ornament on her head. Apart from her corset and petticoat she wore only a simple dress of muslin draped about her in the manner of a Greek statue.' Sallé's search for narrative good sense had led her to break with every convention of stage dress – ballerinas and *premiers danseurs* at this time still appeared in elaborations of court dress no matter what the subject matter of the ballet – in order to enhance the 'truthfulness' of her dance.

In the autumn of the same year Sallé again returned to London, on this occasion
to appear at the Covent Garden Theatre where she was to work with George Frederic
Handel, dancing in his opera *Il Pastor Fido*, and in the following April she danced in his
Alcina, which included a ballet that she had devised herself (although her appearance as
a male cupid, in male dress, was hissed by the audience). Returning to Paris in 1735,
Sallé knew one of her greatest successes when she appeared in Rameau's opera, *Les
Indes Galantes*. Interestingly (a point that Cyril Beaumont has made), many of Sallé's
most celebrated roles were in *pas de deux* in which there was the possibility of
emotional interplay with her male partner. In the following year there came further
renown when she danced in Campra's *L'Europe Galante*. The contemporary historian
Cahusac noted that 'one reads in her expression a whole range of emotions; one saw
her hesitating between fear and hope' in a love scene, an indication of her power to
infuse an emotional richness into her dancing, a rare achievement for the time. Then,
in 1738, at the height of her success, Marie Sallé asked for permission to retire from
the Opéra stage. She continued, however, to appear intermittently in the court theatre
at Versailles for another fifteen years, performing there for the last time three years

*Marie Sallé, in an engraving after Lancret. She has
been transported into an imagined pastoral scene.*

before her death in 1756. It is ironic that the success of La Barbarina (the Italian virtuoso, Barbara Campanini), who created a furore with her physical charm and her brilliant steps, seems to have hastened Sallé's retirement from the professional stage, as Sallé herself had always sought freedom from the traditional hollow display of steps that was usual in the dance of her time.

It would be idle to pretend that many of the *danseuses* of the eighteenth century were not women of generous morals. The theatre was a happy hunting ground for men in quest of amorous intrigue, for brief as well as for lasting liaisons, and any actress, singer or dancer was thought to be available for any man who could either charm or buy her. Gaetano Vestris, the most admired *danseur* of his day, who dominated European ballet in the middle of the eighteenth century, arrived in France from Florence in the train of his sister Violante, who was a vastly successful courtesan and dancer. A notorious womaniser himself, he passed on to his illegitimate son Auguste his zest for life as well as his brilliance as a dancer. By contrast, Auguste Vestris's celebrated pupil, August Bournonville, who was to become the master of the Royal Danish Ballet in Copenhagen in 1830, was determined that dancers should be thought of as morally decent, and his aim in his ballets was to reveal women as fitting companions for the heroes of his works, and dance itself as a noble calling. His sense of achievement must have been considerable when one of his ballerinas received the Bishop of Copenhagen in her home. Only a hundred years before, dancers and actors were not always buried in hallowed ground, nor were priests willing to give them the rites of the Church.

One such artist, as celebrated for her affairs as for her dancing, was the infinitely beguiling Madeleine Guimard who began her career under the dubious patronage of two court gentlemen. At the age of fifteen she entered the *corps de ballet* of the Comédie Française and then moved to the Paris Opéra, appearing for the first time as a replacement for the ballerina Marie Allard in *Les Fêtes Grecques et Romaines,* in which her charms and lightness were much admired. By the following year Guimard featured in the ranks of the Opéra Ballet and was well advanced in her career as a courtesan: police records note that in 1763 she ended an affair with the Russian Ambassador to Spain (then resident in Paris) and took up with the Comte de Rochefort, who gave her 'a pair of ear-rings and a diamond necklace of the greatest value'. In April of the same year she bore a daughter by Jean de la Borde, Governor of the Louvre and first gentleman of the king's bedchamber. Despite accidents, her career flourished. (It is recorded that, when a piece of stage scenery fell on her, thereby breaking her arm, a Mass was said in Notre Dame for her recovery.) On stage Guimard took increasingly important roles; off stage she became, in 1768, the mistress of the Prince de Soubise, who had long treated the Opéra as his seraglio, and now undertook to pay Guimard 2000 crowns per month, while also keeping her in extreme luxury.

The equally wealthy Monsieur de la Borde was providing her with a regular pension as well, but Guimard spent money as merrily as she received it. She gave three dinners a week in her Paris residence: the first for the greatest noblemen of the court and for men of circumstance; the second for writers and intellectuals; the third 'a veritable orgy', according to one commentator, to which came the most fetching girls and the most lecherous men, where 'lust and debauchery reached their peak'. She also acquired a country residence, at Pantin in the suburbs of Paris, in which she had her own private theatre, an enchanting and minute auditorium which could seat 234 spectators. Here witty, often lubricious, entertainments were regularly staged for the delight of her guests (there were screened boxes in which respectable court ladies and members of the Church could watch the plays without being seen), and people spoke of the pleasures of 'going to Pantin' much as they would of 'going to Versailles' to attend court. Guimard's expenditure was not all selfish; she is remembered for her acts of charity to the needy of Paris. It is reported that she once distributed among the poor 6000 crowns which she had just received from the Prince de Soubise, and parish priests in the poorer suburbs had occasion to know of her generosity.

Her income became even more considerable when she admitted the Bishop of Orleans, Monsieur de Jarente, as a generous admirer. The extra money he bestowed on her was much needed, because she had decided to have a private house built in the Chaussée d'Antin. This exquisite residence, known as the Temple of Terpsichore, was designed by Le Doux, the king's architect. Its portico, supported by four columns, bore a sculptured group showing Terpsichore (the Muse of Dance) being crowned by Apollo. Behind the columns a relief showed the Muse's triumph, borne in a car drawn by cupids, preceded by bacchantes and fauns and followed by the Graces of choreography. As well as private apartments, this extravagantly pretty little palace had a theatre which seated 500 people. It was, according to one commentator, 'a jewel of architecture and a marvel of decorative taste'.

Its decorations were by the fashionable painter Fragonard, but just as they were being completed the artist quarrelled with Guimard. His revenge, reportedly, was to return to the building one day and, with a few skilled strokes of his brush, he altered the various portraits he had included of the ballerina, turning her smile into a snarl of rage. In December 1772 the Temple of Terpsichore was habitable and Guimard began a series of performances which were to continue the risqué, and sometimes more than risqué, entertainments that she had given at Pantin.

In 1776 Guimard knew one of the greatest theatrical triumphs of her career in the comedy ballet by Maximilien Gardel, *La Chercheuse d'Esprit* (The Seeker After Wit). In her performance, Guimard's ability to charm her audience with her grace and lightness was admired, for these were qualities associated with the *demi-caractère* style. Her playing of the role, like her dancing, was marked by delicacy, wit, and not a little sincerity: appearing as a simple country girl, this infinitely worldly, sophisticated and elegant woman (her taste was as impeccable in her dress as in her surroundings) showed a sweetness of manner that won all hearts. But, if Guimard was still the public's darling, she was a difficult woman to employ. Jean-Georges Noverre, installed as director of the Opéra Ballet in 1776, found her a bitter and effective enemy as a member of a cabal which sought to get him dismissed, and succeeded. Her power in the theatre was such that a report by the director of the Opéra at the time observed that 'the Demoiselle Guimard is the leading *demi-caractère* dancer. Everyone knows her talent and she still looks very young on stage. If she does not have great virtuosity, she compensates through her extreme grace. She is very good for dramatic ballets and pantomimes, she is zealous and works hard, but she is a source of huge expense for the Opéra, where her wishes are followed with as much respect as if she were director. Following her example, the other ballerinas demand costumes and refurbishments at the greatest expense.'

Guimard seemed indestructible. In her fortieth year she was still the reigning ballerina in the *demi-caractère* style, managing to preserve a markedly youthful appearance on stage, despite falling victim to smallpox. She was attacked by the disease in 1783 but, as one wit observed, 'Not even smallpox can scar a rock.' She was, however, unfashionably thin for the time, earning herself the nickname 'the skeleton among the Graces'. A fall downstairs and an injury to her knee did not affect her, but extravagance did, and, in 1786, in order to solve her financial problems, she thought up the scheme of establishing a lottery to sell off the Temple of Terpsichore, disposing of 2500 tickets at 120 livres each (the winner of the lottery made an immediate profit by reselling the house to a banker for nearly double the sum Guimard raised). She

appeared on a couple of occasions in London where she was much fêted, especially by the Duchess of Devonshire who adored dancing, but London also mocked her thinness and a cartoon published during a visit in 1787 depicted her as a dancing skeleton with the inscription 'Mademoiselle G.....d or Grimhard from Paris'.

In 1789 Guimard left the stage. She married the dancer Jean-Etienne Despréaux, fifteen years her junior and, as a condition of the nuptial blessing, both 'had renounced their calling'. Guimard settled down to domesticity with a charming and talented man who was a clever artist, a wit, and the most delightful of companions. Alas, the French Revolution was soon to bring financial problems in the loss of pensions and income, but this did not affect the couple's gaiety of spirit. One evening Despréaux, yielding to the entreaties of their guests, contrived for his wife and himself to dance in public again, but only from the knees down. In the drawing room of their home a curtain rose sufficiently to show their lower legs and feet as Guimard and Despréaux trod once more the triumphant steps of their greatest days. Later still, Guimard, using just two fingers placed on a drum on her lap, would recreate the choreography of her finest roles. On 4 May 1816, Madeleine Guimard died. Her passing was little remarked by a public who could hardly remember her art across the gulf of Revolution, war, Empire and Restoration; her husband, in a letter, provided the most fitting farewell: 'She was always perfect, because she never lost her grace of manner.'

Despite her well-deserved reputation for high living, Madeleine Guimard was famous for her many acts of generosity to the poor. Attended by putti *bearing foodstuffs, the ballerina is shown here visiting the sick, as she did in real life.*

The Romantic Age

The changes which were affecting European thought, and European history, by the end of the eighteenth century – the French Revolution; the Napoleonic wars; the spread of industrialisation – did not at first have any great impact on ballet. Tradition remained secure in such strongholds as the Paris Opéra, and a generation of fine ballerinas emerged, among them Marie Miller Gardel, Emilie Biggotini, Geneviève Gosselin (who was seen to rise up on the very tips of her toes in 1813), in ballets which continued without significant rupture the style of preceding years. In the other arts, however, the wind of Romanticism had already blown old attitudes away: Berlioz's *Symphonie fantastique* and the music of Chopin and Mendelssohn; Géricault's great canvas of 'The Raft of the Medusa' and the paintings of Delacroix; the poetry of Lamartine and Victor Hugo and the popularity of the novels of Sir Walter Scott announced that strong, even violent emotion, ardent sensibilities and passionate introspection were the artistic order of the day. Inevitably, if slightly later than in music, literature, painting and the theatre, the Romantic movement was to affect ballet. As in all the arts, it was a gradual process, but it was to flower, and to be first acknowledged, in the art of one ballerina, Marie Taglioni.

Of all the ballerinas in this book none, not even Anna Pavlova or Alicia Markova, illustrates so potently as Marie Taglioni the idea of the dancer as a creature of the air. It was Taglioni's good fortune that she should take the stage at exactly the right time for an artist of her particular gifts and physique; or perhaps, more truly, we may say that her artistry imposed itself upon an age, serving as a central image for the dance aspirations of the time and establishing an ideal about dancing which continues to haunt the theatre to this day. So long as *La Sylphide* – or indeed *Les Sylphides* – holds the stage, Taglioni will be immortal. Other ballerinas have placed their indelible mark upon great roles. None, save Taglioni, has been enshrined in a manner of dancing, and none so embodies an ideal.

Marie Taglioni was born in 1804, the daughter of the Italian ballet master Filippo Taglioni and his Swedish wife, Sophia Karsten. The itinerant life of a ballet master meant that the family travelled around Europe and that eventually, while Filippo continued his career in various cities, Marie was educated in Paris. She was inevitably placed in a ballet class – dancing was a dynastic matter – but the thin, round-shouldered and by no means pretty child was not a very promising pupil. Her mother's reports of her progress to her absent father did not prepare him for the disappointment he knew when, in 1822, the seventeen-year-old Marie went to Vienna, where he was then ballet master, to make her début as a *danseuse*. He found her unfitted for the stage. In order to repair the massive deficiencies in her training, Filippo Taglioni embarked upon a most arduous system of classes which sought to make capital from what might have seemed Marie's faults, and aimed to turn her every physical quality to its greatest advantage. For as much as six hours a day, Filippo slaved with his daughter on her technique and on her stage presence so as to realise an image that was moulded from her own slender physique and from the dance technique of the period. There started to emerge a young dancer in whom lightness, ease and a modest grace were the indications of a style vastly different from the coquetry and *tours de force* that were the commonplace of female dancers of the time.

Marie Taglioni's way of dancing seemed the embodiment of the new aspirations and ideals of the Romantic muse in dance. Commentators spoke variously of Taglioni's dancing as 'new'. Its novelty, however, was not that of invention but of a development and extension of a style to encompass new feelings and new expression. Within five years of her début, after dancing throughout Europe, Marie and her father were preparing for her appearance at the Paris Opéra, with her brother Paul as her partner. On 23 July 1827, at the age of twenty-three, Marie Taglioni appeared in a variation interpolated into the ballet *Le Sicilien*. The audience realised at once that here was something different in style from what they had known. Making use of a sublimely easy technique, without straining after bravura effects, Taglioni's lightness, the modest grace of her manner, her way of dancing on 'the tips of her toes' as a natural extension of her airy, lovely manner rather than as a means of exciting attention and her demurely charming presence announced a ballerina of the rarest qualities.

August Bournonville, who observed her in his early years in Paris, wrote: 'The more you see this dancer, the more you discover the charm of her dancing, and if the eye of a ballet master is not constantly flattered, the most rigorous ballet lover could not resist her lightness, her ease, and that voluptuous abandon which never ceases to be the true dance of a woman. She is the idol of the public.' And the idol she was to remain for the rest of her career, undisputed queen of the ballet stage for as long as she chose to perform.

It was not for another five years after her Paris début that Taglioni was to find the perfect realisation of her stage identity in the role of the Sylphide with which she is still associated in our minds. In 1831 she had been nominated as the leading ballerina of the Opéra by its very astute new manager, Dr Véron. Among her roles was the dance scene in the third act of Meyerbeer's opera *Robert le Diable*. In this, the ghosts of lapsed nuns are summoned from their graves in a ruined cloister. Led by the Abbess Helena (Taglioni) they danced in the moonlight while the hero of the opera (sung by the tenor Adolphe Nourrit) watched them. The combination of moonlight, spectral dances and mystery caught the imagination of the public – here was a vivid image of the new Romanticism – and it was Nourrit who provided the idea for *La Sylphide* in which Romanticism can be said to have claimed ballet for its own.

Marie Taglioni as the Sylphide, with her brother Paul as the sleeping James, in the celebrated opening pose of La Sylphide. *This oil painting suggests something of the great ballerina's extraordinary impact on the theatrical and artistic world of her age.*

Previous page Marie Taglioni in Deshayes' ballet of 1831, La Bayadère. *The swirl of her gauzy draperies and the idealised representation of her feet give the suggestion that this supreme Romantic ballerina is truly a creature of the air.*

La Sylphide tells of a man obsessed by an unattainable sprite who destroys himself, and the sprite, in his quest to possess her. In it can be seen Romanticism's affection for the supernatural and its unassuaged longings for elusive beauty and love. Here, as in *Robert le Diable,* were the first germs of the moonlit vapours and ethereal beings who would fill the ballet stage for the next twenty years, and in Taglioni's dancing was a way of performing – poetic, seemingly superhuman in its ease, weightlessly graceful – which made the old style of dancing at the Opéra seem dated. It was Taglioni's naturalness which caught the public imagination.

'Imagine our joy one evening', wrote one critic 'when, unsuspecting and by pure chance, like finding a pearl by the roadside, we were presented not with the *danse noble,* the existing style at the Opéra, but with a simple, easy, naturally graceful Taglioni, with a figure of unheard-of elegance, arms of serpentine suppleness and legs to match, and feet like those of an ordinary woman, even though she be a dancer. When we first saw her so much at ease and dancing so happily – she danced like a bird singing – we could not understand it. "Where is the *danse noble?*" asked the old men. The *danse noble* is as foreign to Taglioni's style as natural dancing is to that of her rivals. She uses her hands when she dances! See how she bends her body, how she walks, how she always keeps to the ground! Notice the absence of *pirouettes, entrechats* and other technical difficulties . . . All the *danseuses nobles*, after seeing how she is applauded, have clipped off some of their nobility, just as their ancestors cast off their panniers. They have been using their arms and legs like ordinary mortals, they have even risked splitting their satin corsets by bending their bodies more, while they bend their arms much less since Taglioni.' (Jules Janin, translated by Ivor Guest in his magisterial *The Romantic Ballet in Paris.*)

Her head crowned with the Sylphide's flowers, little wings on her back and her feet in satin slippers (which were unblocked, but filled with cotton wadding to protect and help her toes in the *pointe* work so important in giving an illusion of flight), Marie Taglioni achieved in *La Sylphide* an idealisation of the ballerina. Nothing she would do in the remaining fifteen years of her dancing career, none of the roles in which her father cast her, in variations of this first supernatural creature, none of the ballets which she was to dance all over Europe, as triumphantly in Russia as in London, Paris, Milan and Vienna, could alter this image. Marie Taglioni was an ethereal being whose shoes were bought by Russian balletomanes, cooked in a sauce, and eaten as part of a banquet.

She was without rival, save for the Austrian dancer Fanny Elssler, a rivalry which was first promoted by Dr Véron in a skilfully managed press campaign to boost the box-office returns at the Paris Opéra. He encouraged audiences to divide into Taglion-ists and Elsslerists, noisily disputing the rival claims of their idols. The two ballerinas were diametrically opposed: Taglioni of the air; Elssler of the earth, a passionate contrast to the modest purity of '*Marie pleine de grâce*'. In Elssler's dancing were all those qualities which Taglioni lacked – great physical beauty, sexual allure, and prowess in small beaten steps.

Elssler at the time of their rivalry also had youth on her side. The celebrated chronicler of the Romantic dance, Théophile Gautier, wrote rather briskly about the difference between the two ballerinas when, in 1838, *La Sylphide* was revived at the Opéra. His review of the event is written by a man plainly caught by the charms of Fanny Elssler and his descriptions are less than just in their implied comments on the other ballerina. He makes the point that Elssler 'is the dancer for men, as Mlle Taglioni was the dancer for women' with a cruel contrast of present and past tense: 'When Fanny dances one thinks of a thousand pleasant things ... you feel yourself leaning on your elbow on the balustrade of a terrace, with roses round your head, a cup full of Syracusan wine in your hand, a white greyhound at your feet, and beside you a beautiful woman with a plumed head-dress and a robe of crimson velvet; you hear the thrum of tambourines and the silvery tinkle of small bells. Mlle Taglioni reminded you of cool and shaded valleys where a white vision suddenly emerges from the bark of an oak to greet the eyes of a young, surprised and blushing shepherd ... If one may make use of the expression, Mlle Taglioni is a Christian dancer, Mlle Fanny Elssler is a Pagan dancer.'

Fanny Essler in her most famous role as the gypsy girl in La Esmeralda, *seen here, in a drawing by Paul Burde, with her faithful goat. The letters with which she has spelled out the name of her beloved Phoebus can be made out in the bottom right-hand corner.*

The final glorious blaze of Taglioni's career came in London in the mid-1840s. Jules Perrot, one of the great dancers of the Romantic age and a choreographic genius, had been resident in London since 1842 as choreographer at Her Majesty's Theatre. Here he was to produce a succession of major ballets which featured four of the leading stars of the golden age of dancing: Fanny Elssler, Fanny Cerrito, Lucile Grahn and Carlotta Grisi, as well as Taglioni. Benjamin Lumley, manager of Her Majesty's Theatre, had in 1843 succeeded in bringing together two of these stellar figures, Elssler and Cerrito, in a *pas de deux* which Perrot had skilfully devised at the express request of Queen Victoria. Two years later Lumley was seized with the apparently preposterous design of uniting four of the greatest stars in a *pas de quatre*, and thus Jules Perrot was presented with the problem of devising a quartet for Marie Taglioni, Fanny Cerrito, Carlotta Grisi and Lucile Grahn in which each artist would be shown off to greatest advantage without for a moment detracting from the qualities of her companions and rivals. The four stars agreed to appear together and rehearsals were set in motion. There was no doubt that pride of place in groupings and seniority in appearance on stage had to be accorded to Taglioni; no doubt either that Lucile Grahn, the newest arrival on the London ballet scene, should take the junior position, but how to decide between the rival claims of Cerrito and Grisi? Perrot was in despair until Lumley came up with an answer: the elder of the two should take her rightful position as second to Taglioni.

'The ladies', wrote Lumley, 'tittered, laughed, drew back and were now as much disinclined to accept the right of position as they had been before eager to claim it. The ruse succeeded. The management of affairs was left in Monsieur Perrot's hands. The order of the ladies being settled, the grand *Pas de Quatre* was finally performed on the same night before a delighted audience, who little knew how nearly they had been deprived of their expected treat.'

On her retirement from the stage in 1847 Marie Taglioni went to live in Italy. She had, in 1832, married the graceless Comte Gilbert de Voisins, but the union proved disastrous and he was not the father of either her son or her daughter. Taglioni was, however, to return to Paris in 1858 to see a young ballerina, Emma Livry, whose début had awoken memories of the first Sylphide, and whose tragic story we tell later. Once in Paris, Taglioni embarked upon a new career as *Inspectrice de la Danse* at the Opéra, and during the next decade was to pass on something of the traditions she had inherited from her father and had so enhanced by her own dancing. Alas, the Franco-Prussian war of 1870 wiped out her investments, and reduced circumstances forced her to return to work, teaching deportment and social dancing in London. At a house in Connaught Square Taglioni instructed well-born young girls, including Princess May of Teck, later to become Queen Mary. More than half a century later Queen Mary could still demonstrate, as she did for the benefit of Dame Adeline Genée, the Danish ballerina, some of the steps she had learned from Taglioni. For the last four years of her life Marie Taglioni lived quietly with her son's family in Marseille. She died the day before her eightieth birthday.

Above *The famous Pas de Quatre, in
the lithograph by T.H. Maguire from
a drawing by A.E. Chalon, 1845.
From left to right we see Carlotta
Grisi, Marie Taglioni, Lucile Grahn
and Fanny Cerrito.*
Left *A lithograph by Brandard which
shows Carlotta Grisi, the first Giselle,
in her transfiguration as a Wili in the
second act of the ballet – a lovely picture
which echoes Gautier's description of
Grisi: 'The apparition flutters
coquettishly. . . . flies towards the reeds
and willows'.*

Next to Taglioni, in discussion of the greatest luminaries of the Romantic dance, as represented by the members of Perrot's *Pas de Quatre,* must stand Carlotta Grisi, creator of *Giselle.*The Grisi family was Italian and musical: Carlotta's cousins were the operatic stars Ernesta and Giulia Grisi; her sisters sang and Carlotta herself is noted as having 'a pretty voice for a dancer' (she even sang in some of her early performances). As a child she was placed in dancing classes in Milan, but the crucial moment in her life came in 1833 when she was working in Naples. At the age of fourteen, bewitchingly pretty with golden-auburn hair, she captivated the dancer and ballet master Jules Perrot, not only by her beauty but also by the evident promise of her dancing. It was the start of a liaison in which she was at first his pupil, then his mistress – for a time she called herself Madame Perrot, although there is no evidence that they were legally married. Guided and trained by Perrot, Grisi embarked on a series of tours throughout Europe during which her technique and stage presence were perfected. The couple won plaudits for their performances when they danced together, although as Carlotta was later to confess, 'The most ardent caress was when Jules stood on my hips like the Colossus of Rhodes while I lay face downwards on the floor – this was to strengthen my hips.'

At last, in 1840, the couple was ready to face Paris. They appeared in the opera *Le Zingaro* (in which Carlotta also sang) at the Théâtre de la Renaissance and from there it was only a matter of time, and some politics, before Carlotta was engaged at the Opéra. During the 1830s Perrot had been a star dancer there, rivalling Taglioni in public acclaim, much to her annoyance. Now he was to make his influence felt as choreographer for Grisi's dances. Her first appearance was in Donizetti's opera *La Favorita,* when her lightness and her 'manner of bounding in the air and alighting softly' won many hearts. A new ballet was planned for her, but fate and the poet Théophile Gautier stepped in. He had fallen wholly under the spell of Carlotta's beauty and charm and was destined to love her unavailingly all his life; his last word was said to be 'Carlotta'. In the spring of 1841, soon after meeting her, the poet conceived a work which he first called *Les Wilis* whose heroine was eventually to be named Giselle.

The choreography for the new ballet, *Giselle,* was entrusted to Jean Coralli, the first ballet master at the Opéra, but it soon became apparent that Perrot was to have a considerable hand in the piece. Adolphe Adam was commissioned to provide the score and, because of his friendship with Perrot and Carlotta, 'the ballet was almost composed' in his drawing room: it was accepted that all Carlotta's scenes were created by Perrot. Preparations for *Giselle* went ahead with all speed and on 28 June 1841, Carlotta's twenty-second birthday, *Giselle* eventually took the stage. Its triumph was complete. Writing of it two weeks later for *La Presse,* of which he was theatre critic, Gautier cast his review in the form of a letter addressed to the German poet Heinrich Heine. He recounted something of the genesis of the ballet, described the plot and concluded with some general remarks about the performance: 'Carlotta danced with a perfection, a lightness, a boldness and a chaste and refined seductiveness which places her in the first rank, between Elssler and Taglioni. As for pantomime, she exceeded all expectations; not a single conventional gesture, not one false movement; she was nature and artlessness personified.'

In *Giselle* we see one of the supreme examples of the art of the Romantic dance, and one of the imperishable vehicles for the art of the ballerina. The first act, in which a simple and sweet young girl is betrayed by a noble lover and then driven mad so that she dies of a broken heart, calls for an actress capable of exposing the emotional side of Romanticism. In the second act the heroine is translated into one of the avenging night dancers, the Wilis, who hunt men down and dance them to their death as revenge for their earthly sufferings – an example of Romanticism's moonlight and mystery. The ballerina here is a creature torn in two, since her nature as a Wili must force her to seek the death of Albrecht (who betrayed her in the first act), while her love for him has transcended death and she must therefore also seek to preserve him from his fate. It is this wonderful contrast, as well as the superb dramatic opportunities of the role, which has helped to preserve *Giselle* for nearly 150 years and has caused ballerinas to revere 'this holy ballet', as Tamara Karsavina, the illustrious Russian ballerina, called it, as one of the supreme challenges of their art.

The success of *Giselle* launched Carlotta as the new star of the ballet in Paris and London. Her list of roles includes such enduring works as *Paquita,* at the Paris Opéra, and *La Esmeralda,* one of Perrot's greatest dramatic masterpieces, in London in 1844. In both Paris and London Grisi appeared in *La Péri,* a work in which she was subjected to a 'make or break' challenge at every performance. The action of the story required that at one moment Grisi, as the Persian fairy of the title, should leap from a platform several feet above the stage into the arms of her partner, Lucien Petipa. 'The *pas* includes a certain fall which will soon be as famous as the Niagara Falls. The audience waits for it with awed curiosity. At the moment when the vision is about to end, the Péri falls from the top of a cloud into her lover's arms,' wrote Gautier. The dangers of the action were obvious and hair-raising. Parisian and London audiences observed the spectacle with very different attitudes, as Ivor Guest has pointed out: at the Opéra, Grisi, having muffed the jump, was forced to repeat it three times before the public was satisfied. In London, under similar circumstances, the Drury audience 'begged her not to risk it' while one devotee 'attended every performance, convinced that the leap would one evening prove fatal, and was eager to be present at the ballerina's demise'.

Carlotta Grisi's participation in the *Pas de Quatre* was followed by roles in two of the three divertissements which Perrot also staged in London as vehicles for the ballerinas (Arthur St Léon, the choreographer and dancer, who became the husband of the ballerina Fanny Cerrito, went so far as to call them 'steeple-chases'). In 1846 *The Judgement of Paris* featured Taglioni, Cerrito and Lucile Grahn; in 1847 *The Elements* starred Grisi, Cerrito and the new ballerina, Carolina Rosati; while finally in 1848 *The Four Seasons* brought together Grisi, Cerrito, Rosati and the young Marie Taglioni, the greater Taglioni's niece.

More success awaited Grisi in Paris, and then, eventually, there came the visit to Russia. The European public, and in particular the London public, by now following the rapturous operatic successes of Jenny Lind, the Swedish nightingale, was tiring of ballet. Russia still beckoned and Grisi was reunited there with Perrot, now ballet master in St Petersburg. Between 1850 and 1853 she danced in Perrot's ballets and was occasionally partnered by him, not least in *Giselle*. But her career was waning and a liaison with Prince Radziwill brought her possession of a handsome property in Switzerland, at St Jean near Geneva. At the age of thirty-five Carlotta Grisi bore Prince Radziwill a daughter, Ernestine, and she retired to motherhood and a quiet and agreeable life at St Jean, much caught up with embroidery and with receiving visits from the ever-devoted Gautier. She married her daughter well, and in 1899 – the glories of the Romantic ballet now long past and *Giselle* only honoured in Russia (the ballet was forgotten in Paris) – Gautier's 'lady of the violet eyes' died.

Fanny Cerrito, Grisi's contemporary and rival ('I dance a good deal with Cerrito, which she does not like, though it pleases me,' wrote Grisi about *The Elements,* one of Perrot's steeple-chases) was even longer lived. Born two years before Grisi, in 1817, she did not die until the spring of 1909 in Paris. The darling of the Romantic age, and London's especial favourite, she was to breathe her last, in her ninety-second year, just as Serge Diaghilev was on the eve of opening his first Russian season in Paris. Another golden age of ballet was on its way, as fascinating as that in which Cerrito had participated seventy years before, but now bringing with it the dancers Pavlova, Karsavina and Nijinsky. And just as this early interpreter of the Sylphide passed from the world, Pavlova and Karsavina were about to evoke her long-forgotten and ethereal style in Fokine's *Les Sylphides.*

Born in Naples in 1817, the tiny, vivacious and dazzling Fanny Cerrito was already acclaimed as a ballerina in Italy while still in her mid-teens. Success followed in Vienna, where she met and worked with Perrot, and then at La Scala, Milan, where she astounded the public and critics by her delicate charm and by her exceptional force of physical skill. It was in 1840 that Fanny Cerrito was invited to appear in London, and the city took her to its heart as 'one of the most gifted dancers in Europe'. There ensued a rivalry with Taglioni, who had returned to London in the summer of 1840, in which the elder ballerina did not win all the commendation. To chaperone her, Cerrito had the slightly preposterous figure of her father, Don Raffaele, who, like the ballet mothers of a later age, was obsessed with his daughter's greatness and is said to have stuffed his pockets with her old shoes and offers from adoring swains.

It is no exaggeration to say that Fanny enslaved London. She captivated society and was received by many of the greatest ladies, while at the same time surrounding herself with an admiring horde of noblemen, including the Duke of Beaufort and the Earl of Cardigan (later to lead the Charge of the Light Brigade). She challenged Taglioni as La Sylphide, appeared in *Le Lac des fées*, and in 1842 tried her hand at choreography, with sufficient success to be entrusted with the creation of the ballet

Above *The pages of the* Illustrated London News *provide a fascinating record of the heyday of the Romantic ballet in London during the 1840s, and this engraving of Fanny Cerrito in the Shadow Dance from* Ondine *captures with especial vividness the moment in which the water sprite first dances with her own shadow. It was from such descriptions that Frederick Ashton was to bring this dance to life again in his* Ondine *of 1958.*

Left *A portrait of Fanny Cerrito shows her in the formal splendour of social dress, but cannot disguise the bewitching charm of her expression.*

Alma at Her Majesty's Theatre, with Jules Perrot as her collaborator. It was this work which established Perrot in London as a choreographer. It also established Cerrito as one of his favourite artists, as his association with Grisi began to wane.

In 1843 Perrot created *Ondine* for Cerrito, in which she appeared in the celebrated Shadow Dance, and in the summer of that year Queen Victoria fell victim to the current fashion for ballet, and for Cerrito in particular, when she expressed a wish to see Cerrito and Fanny Elssler in a *pas de deux*. Although Perrot had only a few days in which to create it, the work was a sensation, allowing Elssler to display all her *terre à terre* brilliance in small beaten steps and *pointe* work, and Cerrito to bound and fly over the stage in the fashion which so characterised her dancing. As we have seen, it was this performance that led the way to the famous *Pas de Quatre* two years later.

By now Cerrito had acquired another suitor, far removed from the aristocrats who haunted the stage boxes and applauded her every move. This was Arthur St Léon, the choreographer and dancer whom she married after an Italian tour in 1845. Back in London, her association with Perrot continued and, following the *Pas de Quatre*, she appeared in his grand Indian ballet *Lalla Rookh,* and in *The Judgement of Paris.* Then, in 1847, Cerrito and St Léon decided to leave London and move to Paris. As the new star of the Opéra, Cerrito bewitched audiences with her speed and her artless bravura, and 'flew like a bird'. Although she worked in Italy and in London as well, between 1848 and 1851 the Paris Opéra was to claim the lion's share of her time. She continued to be partnered by St Léon, not least in the ballet *Le Violin du Diable* which he not only choreographed, but also danced in and played the violin. By 1851, however, the marriage was failing; Fanny Cerrito met the Spanish grandee the Marquis de Bedmar by whom she was to have a child, Mathilde. She returned to dancing, appearing in Vienna and in Paris, where she staged her own ballet *Gemma,* and also ventured to Russia. In 1857 she gave her farewell appearances, very properly in London, making her adieux to the stage in the minuet in *Don Giovanni.* She retired to Paris, spending quiet years raising her daughter and living the life of a bourgeoise in Passy.

The fourth member of the famous *Pas de Quatre* was the Danish ballerina Lucile Grahn. Born in 1819, she showed such talent and taste for dancing as a very young child that she was entered into the school of the Royal Danish Ballet and it is there that August Bournonville first saw her, when he came to take up his prominent position in Danish ballet in 1830. Bournonville is one of the central figures in the ballet of the nineteenth century and one of the most lastingly influential to this day. Born in Copenhagen in 1805 he was the son of the French dancer Antoine Bournonville and – like Marie Taglioni – of a Swedish mother. Although he was to benefit from his father's Parisian connections, he was always proud to consider himself a Dane. In 1820, when he was fifteen, he was taken by his father to Paris for dancing lessons with Auguste Vestris, returning four years later for a further period of study. For nearly five years he studied under Vestris in Paris, taking the most careful note of everything he was taught by this great master of the French 'school' of dancing.

Lucile Grahn in Caterina *or* The Bandit's Daughter.
*Grahn is portrayed in this lithograph by Brandard in
the famous* pas stratégique *in which the heroine teaches
the girls of the* corps de ballet *how to present arms.*

This teaching was to be the basis for all Bournonville's subsequent achievements when he eventually returned to Copenhagen to become ballet master, choreographer and principal dancer and teacher of the Royal Danish Ballet. The Bournonville inheritance – of ballets and of a teaching method – has been preserved and elaborated in Copenhagen and it provides one of the most fascinating insights into the dance of the nineteenth century as well as still being one of the most rewarding means of instruction for dancers today.

The young Lucile Grahn was to have the inestimable benefit of Bournonville's instruction from the age of eleven, and Bournonville was inspired by his admiration of Marie Taglioni – his 'ideal dancer' – to shape his pupil's undoubted gifts. When she was fifteen he took Lucile (with her mother as chaperone) to Paris so that the girl might see Taglioni as La Sylphide. A year later in Copenhagen he staged the ballet *Valdemar*, in which Lucile appeared just after her sixteenth birthday, and after some soul searching – because he did not approve of the extravagant Romanticism of the theme – he decided in 1836 to restage *La Sylphide*. In this production (which is preserved with remarkable faithfulness by the Danish Ballet to this day) Bournonville sought to shape and display the gifts of his young protégée, with whom he had fallen in love. Lucile may have been flattered by his affections but she could not reciprocate them and, after some stormy passages in their relationship, Lucile Grahn eventually felt it necessary to leave Denmark permanently. She had studied briefly in Paris and had known some first successes in Germany; now she determined to escape from the small world of the Danish ballet to the greater opportunities that were promised by an international career.

For the next decade she followed the usual round of the star ballerinas of this period. She danced throughout Europe as far as Russia, where her triumphs were sufficient to arouse the jealousy of the resident ballerinas and, it was suggested, curtailed her engagements because the St Petersburg ballerina Yelena Andreyanova, mistress of the director of the Imperial Theatres, would brook no rival. Grahn's most consider-able successes were undoubtedly those she knew in London, where – like Cerrito – she was to benefit from the presence of the choreographer Jules Perrot. As pupils of Auguste Vestris, both Perrot and Bournonville were concerned to create a dramatic credibility in their ballets. Thus Grahn's education in Copenhagen prepared her for the roles she would find with Perrot, and in *Eoline,* his creation for her of 1845, she provided 'the most graceful dancing with the most soul despairing pantomime'.

In 1846 she starred in Perrot's *Catarina or The Bandit's Daughter* and was very effective in the *pas stratégique* in which the heroine Catarina drills some *danseuses* in military evolution. One critic found it fascinating 'to watch her countenance as she falls into the successive poses' of this dance. 'There is a quite confident intelligence in her face which shows that she not only executes them as a *danseuse* but understands the situation as an actress.'

In these few comments we have a clear indication of that quality which has marked the entire tradition of Danish performance: the quest for dramatic truth as well as for technical efficiency. Grahn was not a great virtuoso, but her dancing was well rounded and always charming. In Bournonville's own ballets he sought to show his female characters as women of moral rectitude and physical sweetness. Although Grahn left the Danish Ballet early in her career, she nevertheless retained many of its attitudes, in her private life as well as in her stage personality.

As the Romantic ballet lost its impetus in London, Grahn found increasing opportunities for her art in Germany, dancing in Hamburg, Leipzig and Munich. In 1856 she retired from dancing and married the operatic tenor Friedrich Young. Two years later, she became ballet mistress in Leipzig where she staged the ballet scenes in the operas produced there. Her marriage suffered when her husband was dreadfully injured in a fall – he remained an invalid for nearly thirty years – and Grahn later worked as ballet mistress in the Munich Court Theatre, staging dance scenes and divertissements in Wagner's operas. She did not die until 1907 and she is remembered in Munich by the street named after her, Lucile Grahnstrasse.

The other side of the Romantic dance is to be found in the art of the Viennese ballerina, Fanny Elssler. She was born in Vienna in 1810; her father had been Haydn's music copyist and valet. The young Fanny was an enchantingly pretty girl who began her career as a child dancer, following in the footsteps of her elder and much taller sister Thérèse (later to be seen in breeches roles when playing opposite her sister). At the age of fourteen Fanny went to Naples as a dancer, and three years later became the mistress of the Prince of Salerno, to whom she bore a son. Three years later, while in Berlin, she bore a daughter, Thérèse, to a dancer, Anton Stuhlmüller. These emotional adventures behind her, she and her sister Thérèse arrived in London in 1833 where they were eventually visited by Dr Véron, then running the Paris Opéra with considerable success and acumen, building upon the triumphs there of Marie Taglioni with the ballet public. As we have seen, Véron, whose business sense was second to none, realised that he might further capitalise on the mania for Taglioni by promoting Fanny Elssler as a rival.

In June 1836 *Le Diable Boiteux* provided Elssler with a solo with which her name has been associated ever since. This was the Cachucha, based on a Spanish dance. Théophile Gautier, describing Elssler's performance, gives a most vivid picture of the charms that conquered audiences in Europe and, later, in America: 'She comes forward in her pink satin *basquine* trimmed with wide flounces of black lace. Her skirt weighted at the hem fits tightly over the hips; her slender waist boldly arches and causes the diamond ornament on her bodice to glitter; her leg, smooth as marble, gleams through the frail mesh of her silk stocking; and her little foot at rest seems but to await the signal of the music. How charming she is with her big comb, the rose behind her ear, her lustrous eyes and her sparkling smile! At the tips of her rosy fingers quiver ebony castanets. Now she darts forward; the castanets begin their sonorous chatter. With her hand she seems to shake down great clusters of rhythm. How she twists, how she bends! What fire! What voluptuousness! What precision!' (*The Romantic Ballet as seen by Théophile Gautier,* translated by C. W. Beaumont.)

This vivid portrait tells everything of the young Elssler's art, and in the following years the flowering of her genius in ballets as diverse as *La Fille mal gardée* and the melodramatic *La Gypsy* fired the imagination of the whole of Europe as audience after audience realised they were in the presence of a consummate dance actress. It was in 1840 that she undertook what must have seemed a daunting enterprise: a tour of America. What was to start out as a reasonably short visit during leave taken from the Opéra – to which she was contracted – developed into a two-year triumphal progress, from New York to Cuba, which brought her not only acclaim but a fortune. Typical of her success was the fact that in Washington Congress suspended its deliberations so that the Government might witness her performance. Her art transcended every difficulty, even in Havana where the grotesque *corps* consisted of swarthy and untrained ladies whose stage appearance was the only thing to interrupt their cigar smoking.

Elssler returned exhausted to Europe, but despite her being barred from the Paris Opéra, which refused to overlook her breach of contract, the next decade brought her success such as she had never known before. In 1843 she undertook for the first time the role of Giselle, a part on which she left a very clear imprint. In Carlotta Grisi's interpretation the mad-scene at the end of the first act had been a largely danced incident. It was Elssler who stressed its mimetic and dramatic power, thus establishing a tradition which has endured through ballerina performance until today, and her Giselle was greeted with the accolade, 'acting of the highest kind'. During Perrot's important six years from 1842–8 as a choreographer in London, Elssler followed her appearance with Cerrito in his *pas de deux* with a radiant performance in *La Esmeralda* in which Grisi also starred. But the culminating and crowning performances of her career were those given in 1849 and 1850 in Russia, where she galvanised the public in St Petersburg and Moscow and was hailed as 'a supreme actress'.

It is not without significance that Moscow, whose ballet public had always had a preference for dramatic performance, found in Elssler an ideal artist, and her performances in 1850 in that city aroused the strongest enthusiasm. Her Giselle was thought sublime, and her farewell performance at the Bolshoi Theatre in *La Esmeralda* brought her 300 bouquets, forty-two curtain calls and – that ultimate accolade for the ballerina – the horses were unhitched from her carriage, which was then drawn through the streets by admiring young men.

In 1851, aged nearly forty-one, Fanny Elssler gave her farewell performance in Vienna. She died in November 1884, barely six months after her great rival, Marie Taglioni. Her later years were marred by the deaths of her two illegitimate children, but the wise investment of the fortune she had made in America ensured that her retirement was spent in comfort and security, in contrast to the financial difficulties that surrounded Taglioni's last years.

A caricature of 1840 which shows Fanny Elssler's arrival in Baltimore, on her magnificent two-year tour of America. She is surrounded by what the caricaturist evidently felt was a crowd of donkeys, and there is a dreadful pun implicit in Fanny's statement, 'I shall remember you for long years'.

Victims

The history of ballet is marked at many points by the tragedy of a talented dancer dying before youthful promise could flower into magnificence. Some ballerinas have died soon after their début, but have nevertheless left an indelible imprint upon their time. The young Russian ballerina, Marie Danilova, one of the loveliest talents to have emerged from the St Petersburg School, was among these. She had her first success in 1808 when she was only fifteen, and within two years had died of consumption. From the middle of the nineteenth century, three ballerinas in particular are remembered whose promising careers were cut short by disease and accident: Adèle Grantzow, Emma Livry and Giuseppina Bozzacchi.

Born in 1845 in Brunswick in north Germany, the daughter of a ballet master, Adèle Grantzow's early promise led to her making her début in the *corps de ballet* in Hanover and then to the chance of working in Paris with the celebrated teacher, Mme Dominique. Here she attracted the attention of the choreographer Arthur St Léon and in 1865, when she was only twenty and still almost completely without stage experience, he arranged for her to make her début as a ballerina on the Bolshoi stage in Moscow in his ballet *Fiammetta*. St Léon was obsessed with this 'merry little girl who possesses everything'. In a letter to the director of the Paris Opéra he wrote, 'In the interests of truth I must say that I have never seen a talent more complete, and so varied and excellent in every style. Her appearance in the evening is charming and I thought of your words when I heard people say yesterday, "She is like the young Elssler." Yes, but Elssler never had her suppleness or her *ballon,* and she has in addition amazing *pointes, tacqueté, batterie,* an expressiveness in her miming and her dancing worthy of a great artist, and a confidence as if she had played in grand ballets for twenty years.'

Success followed success. St Léon arranged for Grantzow to make her Paris Opéra début in *Giselle* and engaged himself to prepare new ballets for her both in Paris and in St Petersburg and Moscow. Despite intermittent illness, the acclaim she received was unprecedented since Elssler's triumphs in Russia, and St Léon could report on 'her delicacy, intelligence and grace'. As a culminating gift for her he had planned the ballet *Coppélia,* but it was now that illness threw its shadow across her career. In 1869 she became too ill to rehearse the role (the Paris Opéra discovered a fifteen-year-old student, Giuseppina Bozzacchi, to replace her) and a year later – the year of *Coppélia*'s triumphant début – the choreographer was dead and Grantzow had developed typhus. Without St Léon to guide her career, she continued to dance in

Russia under Petipa, creating the leading role in *La Camargo*. But her health remained uncertain, and in 1877 her leg became infected. Such was the medical treatment in those days that the infection grew worse, and amputation, that cruellest of fates for a dancer, preceded her death at the age of thirty-two.

Théophile Gautier had been present in the Paris Opéra on the night that Grantzow

*A Russian illustration showing Adèle Grantzow
surrounded by vignette photographs of her most
famous roles in St Petersburg.*
Previous page Emmy Livry *in* Le Papillon.

danced the role of Giselle. He wrote to Carlotta Grisi, the first Giselle, for whom he had conceived the work twenty-five years before: 'I took Estelle [his daughter] to see *Giselle* danced by Mlle Grantzow. She who had not seen the only, the true and incomparable Giselle, the Giselle with golden hair and violet eyes, was very pleased with this one, despite her black hair and eyes. For myself, no one will ever dance Giselle; but, really, Mlle Grantzow is the one who has least upset me in a role that you made so charming, so tender, so touching, so poetic, so impossible for future generations.'

Another victim was Emma Livry, who was destined by fate to dance. But like the butterfly she so unforgettably recreated in the role specially devised for her by Taglioni, she was the creature of a brief and glorious summer before her tragic death from burns, incurred when her skirt caught fire (a danger that has traditionally haunted dancers – even in our time the ballerina Janine Charrat was terribly injured in this way). Born in 1842, Livry was the daughter of the *danseuse* Célestine Emarot and the Baron de Chassiron, a member of the Jockey Club and an habitué of the Foyer de la Danse, that market of available balletic talent at the Paris Opéra. The child possessed a slender but true physique which seemed to suit her for the dance. Like Grantzow, she was sent to classes with Mme Dominique where her progress was sufficiently remarkable to make her mother's new protector, the Marquis de Montguyon, decide that little Emma should make her début, not in the *corps de ballet*, or under any ordinary circumstances, but in a revival of *La Sylphide*, a ballet that (although she was no beauty) would show off her lightness and her delicate charm.

Montguyon's connections were sufficient to ensure that the sixteen-year-old Emma – whose stage name was changed to Livry – should have special treatment. Anticipatory notes appeared in the newspapers to herald the appearance of this new Taglioni, and approaches were made to inveigle the great ballerina herself from her retirement on Lake Como to see this new star perform the role she had created.

Expectations were justified. In her 1858 début as the Sylphide, Livry fulfilled every hope that had been entertained for her: the combination of her lightness, *ballon,* the charming fluidity of her movement and the delicacy of her physique spoke to connoisseurs of the return of Taglioni's style of ethereal beauty. Here was the dancer who it was hoped could recapture the crown from the virtuoso Italian ballerinas who were now dominating the Paris Opéra stage. When Taglioni finally appeared in Paris to see the young Livry she was enchanted, and is reported to have said, 'It is true I never saw myself dance, but I must have danced like her.' Of all her precious gifts, Livry treasured most the portrait Taglioni sent to her which was inscribed: 'Make people forget me; but do not forget me.' She created a ballet for Livry, *Le Papillon* (The Butterfly), with music by Offenbach, and whatever its failings as a dramatic work, the piece allowed Livry to shine, and it seems that Taglioni was also to hand on to her protégée something of her own magic.

In November 1862 Livry was attending a dress rehearsal of *La Muette de Portici* at the Opéra. Eager to hear the great tenor Mario, Emma came on stage and took up a position on a piece of scenery. Despite the obvious dangers, dancers generally refused to wear tarlatans which had been treated with a flame-proofing chemical because it made them stiff and dingy, and when Emma's skirt brushed against a naked gas jet in the wings, it was instantly aflame. In panic, as the gauzy material flared, Livry ran on to the stage. Within seconds a stage fireman had wrapped her in a blanket and put out the flames, but she was badly burned. Infection set in and after eight and a half months of unimaginable suffering, she died. At her funeral two white butterflies were seen to be hovering over her coffin. A casket in the Paris Opéra Museum contains the charred relics of Livry's costume. It is all that remains of a dancer whose greatness could have altered the course of French ballet, saving it from its impending decline and the empty bravura of the Italian ballerinas.

If poor Adèle Grantzow was cruelly cheated of the leading role of Swanilda in *Coppélia* through illness, the fate of Giuseppina Bozzacchi, who eventually created the part, seems even more tragic. Born in Milan in 1853, she early on demonstrated a delight in movement, and at the age of nine began dancing lessons. Her abilities attracted the attention of Amina Boschetti, principal ballerina of La Scala, who was about to move to Paris as a guest ballerina at the Opéra. The Bozzacchi family decided to follow her so that their young daughter might study dancing there. Boschetti introduced the young Giuseppina into the class of the renowned Mme Dominique.

She soon showed outstanding talent and, when funds were no longer available to continue the lessons, Mme Dominique herself arranged for the Paris Opéra to pay a

small retainer to support the girl and her family. So it was that, when it became obvious that Adèle Grantzow would be too ill to take the role of Swanilda, Perrin, director of the Opéra, recalled the little Italian girl on their doorstep and persuaded St Léon and Léo Delibes, the composer, that she would be able to sustain the part. The poster for the Paris Opéra for 25 May 1870 announced the revival of Weber's opera *Der Freyschütz* and the '*début de Mlle Bozzacchi*' in the first performance of *Coppélia* (audiences were given their money's worth in those days).

Bozzacchi's triumph was unmarred: her simplicity and warmth of temperament, her delight in dancing and the sincerity of her mime won all hearts, and the success of the ballet, with its enchanting score, was instantaneous. In July 1870 France declared war on Prussia, and a month later the Opéra was closed for the duration of hostilities which were to go tragically wrong for France. By the beginning of September the army had surrendered to the Prussians and the Emperor Napoleon III was the enemy's prisoner. Paris was now besieged but, despite the feeling of despair in the city – to which must have been added the sorrow of St Léon's death from a heart attack – Bozzacchi continued with her dance training throughout the autumn. However, financial problems once again threatened the Bozzacchi family, and malnutrition and unhappiness took their toll. Giuseppina fell ill with smallpox and, on the morning of her seventeenth birthday, 23 November 1870, she died. At her funeral service, Delibes improvised on the organ, using themes from the ballet which had brought fame to this enchanting young creature.

Far left *Emma Livry's fatal accident; an engraving which shows the dreadful moment when her dress first caught fire during the rehearsal at the Paris Opéra of* La Muette de Portici.
Left *Giuseppina Bozzacchi as Swanilda in* Coppélia, *photograph, 1870.*

The Italian Virtuosos

Although ballet in Italy did not excite such attention or know such choreographic riches as in Paris, the flood of ballerinas produced by Italy in the last decades of the nineteenth century came to dominate the stage in Paris and other capital cities of Europe, from London to St Petersburg. Leading the invasion were the technically formidable virtuoso *danseuses* shaped by the Milanese School of the great teacher Carlo Blasis and his successors, with the result that Italian technical attitudes began to impose themselves almost everywhere. The French school of dancing had already yielded to the brilliant *tours de force* of such Romantic stars as Fanny Cerrito, Olimpia Priora, Sofia Fuoco and Carolina Rosati, and their successors – Amina Boschetti, Guglielmina Salvoni and Amalia Ferraris – became the queens of the Paris Opéra, swamping the few French talents, from Emma Livry to the enchanting Léontine Beaugrand, beneath a tide of *pirouettes* and *fouettés*.

One reason for this technical virtuosity was that Italian shoemakers led the way in perfecting the blocking which stiffened the toes of the ballerina's shoes. Where French dancers were still using a soft silk slipper which they darned and wadded to provide support for their feet, the Italians already had the added support of the blocked toe shoe which permitted more dazzling *pirouettes* and faster, more sustained *pointe* work. The first records of dancers going 'on *pointe*' can be traced to the early years of the nineteenth century, when the French ballerina Geneviève Gosselin made herself noticed by 'going up on the tips of her toes' at the Paris Opéra. In the 1820s the Italian ballerina Amalia Brugnoli excited considerable attention by this same feat, but it was Marie Taglioni who showed how *pointe* work might be transformed into theatrical art rather than being a physical difficulty merely to be overcome.

Until the middle of the nineteenth century, when Italian shoemakers contrived the breakthrough into stronger shoes, *pointe* work was exclusively the province of the ballerina. The Russian ballerinas of the 1870s and 1880s, Lydia Geiten and Yekaterina Vazem, commented on the change in technique and the loss of an older form of schooling which had been brought about by the Italian shoe and by Italian virtuosity. 'We used to dance in supple shoes, soft all round,' wrote Geiten, 'but the Italian shoe is hard, difficult to bend, so strongly reinforced that it becomes a disgrace, goes out of shape, makes a noise.' Vazem noted: 'In the old ballets the dances were infinitely simpler than they later became, and the *corps de ballet* never worked on *pointe*.' Vazem provides a fascinating insight into the shoes worn by the principal ballerinas of her time, observing that it was Marie S. Petipa, the first wife of Marius Petipa, 'who was the first of our ballerinas to use a double block in the point of her dancing shoes. Before her, ballerinas usually danced without any padding in their shoes. M. S. Petipa, afraid to rely on her weak feet, would put the block from an old pair into her shoes.'

At the Paris Opéra the bravura and vivid charm of the Italian ballerinas quickly supplanted in popular admiration the quiet and more gentle style of what was soon to seem a forgotten 'school': indeed, Léontine Beaugrand, who inherited the role of Swanilda when the Opéra reopened after the Franco–Prussian war and the collapse of the Commune, and again at the inaugural performance at the grand Opera House designed by Garnier in 1875, may be considered the last of a great line of French ballerinas. Another reason for the decline of the French school was the presence at the Eden Theatre in Paris during the next decade of Italian dancers and ballets that rivalled in popularity – and outdid in extravagance – the Opéra repertory.

The first of the new Italian-trained stars was Rosita Mauri who – although Spanish born and partly trained in France – had been polished in Milan. She made her starring début in 1878 in *La Korrigane,* a delightful ballet on a Breton theme, with an excellent score by Widor, which enjoyed enormous popularity at the time. In the same decade Rita Sangalli appeared in one of the finest works that this debased period of French ballet produced, *Namouna,* choreographed by Lucien Petipa, whose score by Edouard

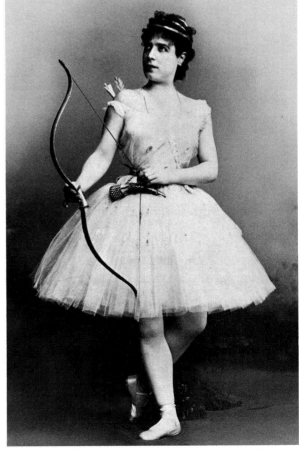

Lalo is one of the greatest in the whole of the nineteenth-century dance repertory. The Italian domination of the Opéra continued when, in 1894, Carlotta Zambelli was engaged as a replacement for Mauri, Zambelli's reign at the Opéra lasting until 1930. The process was reinforced by the arrival of Aida Boni, another product of the Milanese School, as *étoile* in 1908.

There was a long-founded tradition in St Petersburg of inviting guest stars for each season of the Imperial Ballet, dating back to the golden years of Romanticism. During the latter part of the nineteenth century, Italian ballerinas appeared there regularly. Their contribution to the development of Russian ballet at an important moment in its history would be hard to overestimate, and it is Virginia Zucchi who must be credited with having had the most profound and galvanising effect upon the audience in Russia. By means of her artistry and her communicative power as a dance actress, she breathed new life into the most revered items of the repertory and excited extreme public enthusiasm whenever she danced.

Born in Parma in 1849, she demonstrated her dancing ability at an early stage, and was taken by her family to Milan where she trained, although not at La Scala. By the time she was thirty she had danced throughout Italy, gaining a reputation as a prima ballerina of vivid dramatic powers, and she had also danced in Berlin and in

Far left Léontine Beaugrand *was one of the last dancers to represent the gentler French style of performance before the advent of the Italian virtuoso ballerinas. She was blessed with extraordinary elevation and very great charm as a performer. For two decades, in the 1860s and 1870s, she shone at the Opéra, retiring in 1880. She died in Paris in 1925 at the age of 83.*

Centre Rosita Mauri *as Sylvia in the title role of the ballet first staged at the Paris Opéra by Louis Mérante.*

Left Carlotta Zambelli *looking absolutely enchanting in Joseph Hansen's ballet* La Ronde des Saisons *at the Opéra in 1905.*

Previous page Rita Sangalli in Yedda, *a ballet that was inspired by the vogue for things Japanese. Staged at the Paris Opéra in 1879, the choreography was by Louis Mérante to a delightful score by Olivier Métra.*

the opera seasons at Covent Garden. Success followed in Paris, where she appeared in one of the most celebrated balletic extravaganzas of the age, *Sieba,* at the Eden Theatre, into which the choreographer Luigi Manzotti crammed several hundred dancers and elaborate production ideas to dazzle the Paris audience, as he had earlier done with his *Excelsior* at La Scala. Zucchi's gifts as a tragedienne of the dance were now mature and, in such demanding ballets as *La Esmeralda* and *Brahma* and in the comedy *La Fille mal gardée,* she conquered the European public. In 1885 she was invited to appear in St Petersburg on the outskirts of town in one of the summer theatres where the public went to be entertained during the long 'white nights'. Her vehicle was Offenbach's operetta *Le Voyage dans la lune.*

Zucchi was the first Italian ballerina to be seen in St Petersburg for several years and her appearance aroused considerable interest which, within moments of her starting to dance, turned to the most feverish enthusiasm. Her admirers included the critic Skalkovsky who wrote extensively and admiringly about her, not least when he declared, 'There is more poetry in Zucchi's back than in all modern Italian literature.' With her tangled black hair (artfully given to falling into disarray during performance, much to her devotees' delight), Zucchi proved an irresistible dramatic force when the ballet *Brahma,* for long a favourite vehicle of hers, was revived. Her effects astounded the St Petersburg public; memories of both Elssler and Rosati were invoked to suggest how intense was her dramatic presence. Since 1873 the Imperial Theatres had not employed foreign stars. Now Zucchi was invited to appear at the Bolshoi Theatre, St Petersburg, and her performance in November 1885, in Petipa's *Pharoah's Daughter,* aroused unprecedented interest.

Some idea of her effect upon the Russian balletomanes can be gauged from the writings of Alexandre Benois, the painter and designer who was to be instrumental in encouraging Diaghilev's interest in ballet. He fell under the spell of her radiant femininity and her peerless dramatic art and, in the fascinating volume of memoirs which he wrote in 1939, *Reminiscences of the Russian Ballet,* he devotes an entire chapter to 'The Divine Zucchi', recalling with extreme vividness the effect she had made on him fifty-five years before. 'Those who never saw Zucchi can hardly imagine how wonderful it was, but some of our great ballerinas who were afterwards to create the worldwide celebrity of the Russian ballet did actually witness the miracles I have been describing and have preserved an ineffaceable memory of it all. M. F. Kshesinskaya and O. O. Preobrazhenskaya speak of Zucchi, whom they saw in *La Fille mal gardée,* with a profound reverence. There can be no doubt that our great ballerinas were influenced by this example at the beginning of their career; that it played an important part in forming their artistic personality and was transferred through them to the entire Academy of St Petersburg.

'Zucchi's success overwhelmed St Petersburg. The whole town demanded seats in the Bolshoi Theatre, then in its last season. Society talked only of the "divine Virginia" and only to praise her. Still more important was the fact that since Zucchi's success in the autumn of 1885, there was a definite revival of interest among the Russian

Left *Virginia Zucchi as she appeared in*
Brahma *in St Petersburg in 1885. Alexandre
Benois recalled of her performances in this
ballet that 'many spectators were reduced to
tears, and on one occasion two ladies were so
affected that they had to be carried out in a
faint'.*
Below *Pierina Legnani in the second act of*
Swan Lake. *Her pose gives a very good idea
of the style of this greatest of the Italian
virtuoso ballerinas.*

public for the ballet – an interest that has never waned since then and never died. It has outlived even the Bolshevist Revolution.'

Zucchi introduced the Italian fashion for shorter ballet skirts to Russia, insisting that they be cut just above the knee rather than below it, and her prestige seems to have imposed this as a fact rather than a passing mode. Her success paved the way for other Italian ballerinas in summer theatres and at the Mariinsky, but her own career in Russia was to know difficulties. Her contract with the Imperial Ballet was not renewed because of her involvement with a young aristocrat, and when she returned to Russia it was with a touring company which did not provide the proper setting for her art. She went back to Europe, to tour with her company in Italy and to appear in Bayreuth, where she staged the Venusberg scene in Wagner's *Tannhauser* for the 1891 season. In 1892 she made a last return with her troupe to St Petersburg, and though her powers were in decline she could still arouse enthusiasm through the passionate intensity of her mime. For another six years she appeared variously in Europe as mime and dancer, but she gave her final performance in 1898, when she was in her late forties.

When she died in 1930, the Diaghilev Ballet had just ceased its operations following the death of the great impresario. It is possible to trace a very clear link between Diaghilev's work and Zucchi's influence in Russia. Had it not been for her power over the audience, and especially over Alexandre Benois, it is quite conceivable that Benois's interest in ballet would have waned and Diaghilev's never have been kindled.

Of all the other Italian ballerinas,– many of whom were Milan-trained – who appeared in St Petersburg and established the standards of technical prowess that Russian dancers were to seek to emulate, the most significant and the longest lasting in influence was Pierina Legnani. Valerian Svetloff, the great Russian critic, wrote of her: 'She did not shine because of her dramatic temperament, nor her mimetic abilities; nevertheless, our knowledgeable public, who had admired the most celebrated stars from the whole world, was astounded by her virtuosity in the classic style, by the impeccable precision of her steps, and especially in that most difficult feat of virtuosity, the *fouetté*, unknown until then in Russian choreography ... The *fouetté* will remain indissolubly linked with the name of Legnani, who bequeathed it to our Russian ballerinas, among whom Vera Trefilova was, after her, the finest executant on the Mariinsky Theatre stage.'

Born in 1863 in Milan, Legnani studied in her native city with Caterina Beretta, and was nominated prima ballerina at La Scala in 1892. She danced throughout Europe, appearing in London in stagings at the Alhambra Theatre from 1888 to 1892, and then again in 1894 and 1897. It was in London that we have the first printed record of her famous *fouettés* in the ballet *Aladdin*. In a beguiling interview published in the *Sketch* in April 1893, the ballerina (then aged thirty, but who the interviewer says is 'just about twenty-two') discusses her diet which was apparently massive, although her aunt (who accompanied her on all her tours) repeatedly says that she 'eats nothing'. Legnani admits to a 'quite heavy breakfast' of *café au lait* with yolks of egg in it, and fillet of beef or other solid things; then, after a two-hour class, a lunch at 2 pm of 'five or six dishes and some Chianti' and finally, after her rest and her performance, bouillon with egg yolks.

'In the last tableau of *Aladdin*,' she says, discussing her blocked shoes which she shows to the interviewer, 'I turn thirty-two *pirouettes* on tip-toes without dropping my foot.'

Legnani first went as guest ballerina to Russia in 1893, and returned every season until 1901: it was here that she had her most considerable success and influence as an apostle of Italian virtuosity. Her partner in certain ballets was Nikolay Legat, and in his memoirs (*The Story of the Russian School*, published in London in 1932) he notes: 'At her début in the ballet *Cinderella* there was a dramatic pause in the coda. Legnani walked to the centre of the stage, signalled to the conductor, and executed thirty-two *fouettés* on one spot. The feat brought the house down and marked an epoch in the progress of pure technique on our stage.

'To appreciate the overwhelming effect of this purely technical and nowadays [1932] common dancing trick on the balletomane audience of that time, the reader must imagine the atmosphere of the period. It was the period of bloom of Russian art and Russian literature. New schools, new tendencies, new groupings of thought, were springing up on every hand. Every striking new departure was hailed either as a step towards artistic or philosophic liberation by its supporters, or denounced by effervescent critics as a plunge towards perdition. But nothing was received with indifference. In the realm of ballet the Italians had given a tremendous impulse to Russian art by their specific development of technique. Our dancers, male and female, our balletomane critics, even our professors, raved technique and when Legnani, by first performing this hitherto unknown *tour de force*, outdid her own compatriots in their own special sphere, she left both colleagues and spectators stunned.'

Legat understood the mechanics of Legnani's trick, and in time he passed them on to the emergent generation of Russian ballerinas, notably Kschessinskaya, Trefilova, Vil and Vaganova. In Russia Legnani was accorded the supreme accolade of the official title *prima ballerina assoluta*, which she shared with only one other dancer in the entire history of the St Petersburg ballet, M. F. Kschessinskaya. It was a tribute to her prodigious technique and artistry that she was awarded the leading role in several of Marius Petipa's late ballets: *The Talisman, Bluebeard, Raymonda* and *Les Ruses d'Amour*. She is, however, remembered chiefly for her appearance as Odette-Odile in the first St Petersburg production of *Swan Lake* in 1895 in which, in the third act, her *fouettés* were given great dramatic significance as the enchantress Odile dazzles Prince Siegfried.

The Imperial Russian Ballet

The Russian ballerinas of the early and mid-nineteenth century were undoubtedly gifted, but many of them tended to be overshadowed by the glamour surrounding the foreign, and particularly the Italian, guests. One dancer, however, Yekaterina Vazem, preserved the older Russian (more truly, French) style unsullied and was instrumental in passing it on, through her teaching, to the succeeding generations of ballerinas – including Pavlova and Vaganova – who, in the great flowering of Russian ballet at the turn of the century, came to dominate the ballet stage.

Yekaterina Vazem entered the Imperial Ballet School in St Petersburg when Jules Perrot was ballet master there, and she did not die until 1937, by which time Tsarist St Petersburg had become Soviet Leningrad, and the company in which she had seen the last glow of balletic Romanticism was putting on works of such socialist significance as *Partisan Days*. Vazem graduated into the Imperial Ballet in 1867 and soon attracted the attention of Marius Petipa. Petipa, born in Marseille in 1818, had arrived in St Petersburg in 1847 as a *danseur*, and had also started to stage ballets, serving first under Perrot and then St Léon. By 1869 he was nominated first ballet master to the Imperial Ballet, and for more than three decades he was to build a repertory and encourage the expansion of Russian ballet through such grand spectacles as *La Bayadère*, *The Sleeping Beauty* and *Raymonda*, which are but three of the more than fifty works he created. The Petipa repertory is a monumental achievement, the sound foundation of classic academic dance upon which rested (and still rests) the idea of ballet as a theatre art.

For Vazem, Petipa created roles in *The Butterfly* (1874), *La Bayadère* (1877), in which she was the first Nikiya, *The Daughter of the Snows* (1879) and *Zoraya* (1881), as well as the central bravura showcase in the *Grand Pas* which he interpolated into *Paquita* in 1881. She had the most dazzling technique of her time – which is what attracted Petipa to her. In all, she appeared in twenty-two ballets, and critics praised the ease and lightness of her dancing as well as its academic precision. At the end of her life, writing of the changes she had seen on stage in her years as a ballerina, she noted: 'Dance variations differed greatly from those of the later classical ballets, which were influenced by the effective but crude idiom of Italian choreography. Girls rarely danced on *pointes*. The dances were based on small filigree steps, so difficult to perfect, and on little *entrechats*. Outstanding in this respect was St Léon's favourite, the famous ballerina Muravyeva; of her it was said that she could "weave lace with her feet".'

Above *Marfa Muravyeva; an engraving which shows the Imperial Russian ballerina in day dress during her Paris visit of 1863.* Right *Yekaterina Vazem as Catarina in Marius Petipa's revival of Jules Perrot's ballet about the Bandit's Daughter, as staged in St Petersburg. The pose and the costume are not dissimilar to those of Lucile Grahn (see page 41).* Previous page *A portrait photograph taken in St Petersburg of Anna Pavlova which wonderfully conveys the ballerina's ethereal beauty.*

The first Russian ballerina to take up the challenge of the Italian virtuosos was Mathilda Kschessinskaya who was to reign over the stage of the Mariinsky Theatre for a quarter of a century. Born in 1872, the daughter of a celebrated Polish character dancer, she was the pupil of Vazem and of the Swedish Christian Johansson (himself the pupil of Bournonville, who had partnered Taglioni in Paris), and graduated into the Imperial Ballet in 1890. Shortly afterwards she began a liaison with the Tsarevich Nicholas, and was later to become involved with other members of the Imperial family, eventually marrying the Grand Duke André (the Tsar's cousin) after the Revolution. Her friendships brought her considerable power within the company and speedy promotion within its ranks, but her achievement of prima ballerina status in 1896 was allied to a tremendous determination. She worked to rival the virtuosity of Legnani; her own vivid dance personality, her energy and powerful projection helped her to emulate the dramatic effects of Zucchi.

Mathilde Kschessinskaya in her Russian dance. The great ballerina was of Polish origin, and throughout her career she appeared in very stylish folk dances as well as in the pick of the classic repertory. As late as 1936, Arnold Haskell persuaded her to perform this dance at a Covent Garden gala.

In the by now hidebound routine of the old ballet, Kschessinskaya, decked in a king's ransom in diamonds acquired through her royal connections, epitomised the image of the ballerina as the justification for the nineteenth-century ballet. All Petipa's creations, indeed all the ballets since the Romantic age, had served as settings for the art of the ballerina. She was their motive force and their dramatic and technical effects, simple or complex, were designed to show her off as technician, as desirable object and as goddess. Kschessinskaya represents the last fantastic realisation of this trend. Her dancing was marked by academic correctness, strength and technical sparkle. It would soon, to Russian eyes which were to see the lyric emotionalism of Anna Pavlova and the choreographic innovations of Mikhail Fokine, appear old-fashioned and even unreal. Kschessinskaya, who danced until 1915, was the last representative of an old order, both in the theatre and out of it.

The new order was headed by the legendary Anna Pavlova. The details of her

Far left, left and following page
*Pavlova in three of her most famous
roles, in* The Dragonfly *(1915);
as Giselle in the second act of the
ballet; and as the Dying Swan.*

birth and of her parentage are wrapped in some mystery; her date of birth is generally accepted as 12 February 1881. At the age of ten she entered the Imperial Ballet School in St Petersburg and in later years Pavlova herself declared that it was a performance of *The Sleeping Beauty* at the Mariinsky Theatre which inspired her with a desire to dance. If, as has been assumed, she was of humble birth, an education at the Imperial Ballet School would have been in itself a welcome form of security for a child from a poor family. Her artistry began to be formed in the classes of Vazem and of the noble male dancer Pavel Gerdt, and from the time of her graduation at the age of seventeen she seemed marked for greatness. Coached by the former ballerina Evgenia Sokolova and by Christian Johansson, she also sought to acquire the strength of the Italian school by studying with Caterina Beretta, and in due time also obtained the services of Enrico Cecchetti as her private teacher. With her technique thus assured, she was ready to face the greatest challenges of her art.

That she was a uniquely gifted, and uniquely different, artist was evident from her earliest appearances, and the aged Marius Petipa was able to provide roles ideally suited to her youthful genius: Giselle, and Nikiya in *La Bayadère*. In both of these

ballets, where the life of the spirit must shine through the dance, where deception is purged by death and the transmuted soul of the heroine appears as a forgiving, consolatory presence to the hero, Pavlova's art was perhaps most truly revealed. Valerian Svetloff, the eminent Russian critic, wrote: 'The special characteristic of her talent is a sort of immateriality which seems to detach her from anything earthly ... The first performance of *Giselle,* an essentially Romantic ballet, revealed the power of her dramatic talent as well as the lightness of her technical dancing ... Pavlova made this ballet live again on the Russian stage and so inaugurated a new era of Romanticism. Pavlova has succeeded in triumphing over the greatest technical difficulties inherent in the art of dancing itself. Her technique is "soft", intimate, sincere. One does not notice it – not until the variation is near the end and one suddenly realises that it was bristling with difficulties, which only the beauty of the plastic execution has masked until then.' An art critic said enthusiastically after seeing Pavlova dance: 'She is not a woman, she is a museum of poses, of lines, of plastic forms, with a soul. Every single one of her movements should be painted and sculptured as a treasure for posterity. Pavlova has incarnated in herself the spirit of the dance – that is her great glory.'

Pavlova, for all she was nurtured within the protective surroundings of the Imperial Theatres, knew that hers was an individual art and one that dictated its own setting. Thus it was as early as 1907 that she made the first of her tours, to Riga and other northern capitals, as a concert artist. Although she retained her association with the Imperial Ballet for another six years, she had started on the itinerant career that she would follow for the rest of her life. She participated in Diaghilev's first Russian ballet seasons in Paris in 1909, and in London in 1911, but by then she had conquered America with a first visit in 1910 to the Metropolitan Opera House, New York, and had played a London season at the Palace Theatre, as well as touring the English provinces to huge success. By 1912 she had made her permanent home in London. From this base, Ivy House in Golders Green, she was to venture around the world with her own company for two decades, driven inexorably on by her missionary zeal for dance. She inspired a passion for ballet among her audiences, not least in a young English boy in Lima, Peru, who determined to take up dancing as a career and, in time, became Britain's master choreographer, Sir Frederick Ashton.

That Pavlova was one of the greatest geniuses of the dance that the world has ever seen is in no doubt. That she was reactionary in her taste, trusting in the classic dance for her greatest successes, is a commonplace. Her art shunned extremes and was shy of the modern, finding its fullest realisation in such hallowed pieces as *Giselle, Don Quixote* and *The Sleeping Beauty,* and in the multitude of smaller ballets and solos which explored no new horizons in dance but which Pavlova's temperament and artistry kept entirely new.

Pavlova's life was given wholly to dancing. Nothing else seems to have touched her. Of her personal existence, of Pavlova the woman, we know little beyond the conventionalities offered by her husband, Victor Dandré, and by the writings of her admiring collaborators. The paltry films which have survived of her dancing can only hint at her greatness, yet in *The Dying Swan* – the solo which will be for ever associated with her – or the enchantingly mimed *Christmas,* there is no doubt that we are seeing an artist of unparalleled communicative beauty and power. So much else about this ballerina among ballerinas, who drove herself unsparingly to the very last, remains legend. When, at the age of fifty, sick with pleurisy and pneumonia, she lay dying in The Hague, we are told that she whispered a final request for her Swan costume to be brought to her so that she could rekindle for a last moment the spirit that had blazed so brightly before the ballet public. The legend of that spirit still remains, and Pavlova's name still means 'ballet' to people the world over.

Also of the St Petersburg School was Tamara Karsavina. Born in St Petersburg in 1885, the daughter of the dancer Platon Karsavin, she was the pupil of Christian Johansson, Pavel Gerdt and Enrico Cecchetti and entered the Imperial Ballet in 1902. Her enchanting volume of balletic memoirs, *Theatre Street,* charts, with extraordinary freshness, the career of this greatly loved ballerina from the early days of her entry into the Mariinsky Ballet to her gradual ascent of the ladder and her final achievement of ballerina status. It was her involvement in Diaghilev's experimental Ballet Russe, and especially her work in the Fokine repertory, that earned Karsavina immortality: she is the first great ballerina of modern ballet.

Karsavina's beauty was undeniable. Her lustrous dark eyes, the ravishing shape of her head and its beautiful placing on her neck won her attention, although her dancing was not felt to be academically brilliant. She was the ideal interpreter of the roles that Mikhail Fokine created for her. His devotion to her – he was in love with her – ensured that these parts explored, with a lover's perception, the youthful wealth of her talent as well as her exceptional intelligence and expressive grace. As a choreographer Mikhail Fokine was in rebellion against the formal splendours and the elaborate spectacle of the Petipa ballets in which he had danced as a member of the St Petersburg Ballet. By the early years of this century he had formulated ideas for balletic reform, and had started creating his first works in which he sought to break with Petipa's traditions, introducing the new, dramatically expressive ballet. It was his collaboration with Diaghilev which provided the repertory for the early seasons of the Ballet Russe. In Fokine's *Les Sylphides* and *Cléôpatre,* in *Le Carnaval,* and then in her first created role, *The Firebird* (Pavlova had turned down the ballet because she did not approve of Stravinsky's musical modernism), Karsavina became synonymous with the triumphs of the Diaghilev enterprise.

The series of ballets put on by Diaghilev's company, which included the cream of new, young Russian dancers, caused a sensation among Paris audiences in its first season in 1909. Valerian Svetloff wrote later: 'The appearance of Karsavina, with a partner having the power of Nijinsky, had the effect of a revelation in Fokine's *Le Pavillon d'Armide.* I do not think that such applause was ever heard in any other theatre in the world. It even compelled the orchestra to stop playing. And from that day Karsavina was the idol of Paris ... Thus is tradition overthrown ...'

Karsavina in her created role as the Doll in Petrushka *1911.*

In Diaghilev's second season in 1910 Karsavina was seen as Giselle, a role in which her sense of period style and the grace of her manner were much admired, but it was Fokine who again offered her the greatest challenges as the Doll in *Petrushka,* as Thamar, as the Queen in *Le Coq d'Or,* Zobeide in *Schéhérazade* and the Young Girl in *Le Spectre de la rose.*

In this latter piece she was once again partnered by Nijinsky, and Svetloff, describing this celebrated duo, observed: 'The subject is a girl's dream after a ball. She returns, full of naive and innocent fancies, to her bedroom, and over-tired, falls asleep without undressing while still clasping in her hands the rose given to her by her lover. The rising moon can be seen through the big French windows that open upon a mysterious park. All at once the flower is transformed into a youth – a rose-like vision – who draws her into a whirling dance. Then the vision floats through the window and disappears into the garden; while the maiden falls exhausted into a chair. She awakes. At her feet lies a faded rose. That is all . . .

'The simplicity of the music, choreography and poetry may, rendered in dry words, produce scant interest, but in reality, as executed by Nijinsky and Karsavina, the dance is resplendent, dazzling in its beauty; while music, choreography, subject, decoration and costumes (Bakst) all take their place in one artistic whole. There is nothing superfluous in this ballet. Everything is fragrant with subtle and delicate charm. It is most difficult to discriminate between reality and fantasy. Karsavina creates an image of such loveliness that it is not easy to imagine anything more perfect.'

In addition to her romantic roles, Karsavina showed herself willing to participate in the most adventurous works that Diaghilev produced, and she was one of the trio of tennis players in Nijinsky's ultra-modern *Jeux* of 1913. And yet, while starring in all the pre-1914 Diaghilev seasons, Karsavina maintained her position at the Mariinsky Theatre, where she also danced much of the traditional repertory, although she did not excite quite the enthusiasm that she was to know with European audiences.

In 1918 Karsavina left Russia with her second husband, the English diplomatist H. J. Bruce, and their small son, and established herself in London. She returned to work with Diaghilev, creating the role of the Miller's Wife in Massine's *Le Tricorne* in London in 1919, and the leading role of Pimpinella in *Pulcinella,* before undertaking extensive concert tours and returning to Diaghilev yet again for the surreal *Roméo et Juliette* of 1926, in which she was partnered by the young Serge Lifar. Further concert tours and occasional guest appearances in her Diaghilev repertory preceded her retirement in 1931, although not before she had made some late appearances with the infant Ballet Rambert. Thereafter she was to remain much involved in British ballet, a loved and revered figure. She passed on some of the nuances of her roles to Margot Fonteyn, notably those in *Giselle, The Firebird* and *Le Spectre de la Rose,* and also taught Sir Frederick Ashton the delightful mime scene in the second act of *La Fille mal gardée,* when Lise dreams of marriage and motherhood, which Ashton was to incorporate into his new version of the ballet in 1960.

Karsavina died in 1978, and the most fitting comment on her art, which touched many hearts, is that made seventy years before her death by a Russian critic when contributing to a celebratory volume about her: 'Karsavina's dancing is like a sonnet, where every line is a gift to the altar of poetry. Her dancing is the flow of the stream and not that of the angry sea. The lines of her dancing are simple and pure. Simplicity is the ennobling loveliness of Karsavina's creative work, as it is in every art. In this atmosphere bloom the most delicate flowers of the poetry of dancing, which the ballerina – like a fairy flying over woods, valleys, mountains and the sea – distributes to the world.'

The Russian ballerina Olga Spessivtseva is mentioned by those who knew and worked with her in terms of such reverence that it is difficult for the public today to understand quite where her greatness lay. That she was a sublime dancer – for certain people she was *the* supreme dancer of the twentieth century, to be preferred even to Pavlova – there can be no doubt. That she was a tragic figure, one haunted by fate and ill health, is part of the mystery of her art and life.

Born in 1895 in Rostov, Spessivtseva studied at the Imperial School in St Petersburg, graduating in 1912 into the Ballet. From the first, there was some unearthly quality, some beauty hard to define if easy to comprehend, which marked her dancing. Her physique was fragile, her attraction that of a shy creature, and her legs and feet almost extravagantly ideal for classic dancing: ballerinas still speak with enthusiasm of her *développé*, 'like the opening of a flower', and of her flawless lyric-classic style in such ballets as *Giselle* and *Swan Lake*.

She was Diaghilev's favourite classic dancer; when Cecchetti declared that 'God created an apple, of which Pavlova was one half and Spessivtseva the other,' Diaghilev declared that 'Spessivtseva was the half the sun shone on,' and this cannot wholly be dismissed as the barbed comment of a man who had parted company with Pavlova on artistic grounds. Spessivtseva was no less a traditionalist than Pavlova, no less dedicated to the austerities of the classic academic style, and her dancing had the same spiritual illumination, the same sense of having some uniquely powerful and poetic message for the world.

Within four years of entering the ballet at the Mariinsky Theatre, Spessivtseva was nominated a leading soloist. By this time she had already made a first trip abroad, appearing with Diaghilev's company in its American season of 1916–17, and she had even danced with Nijinsky in *Le Spectre de la Rose*. On her return to St Petersburg she was nominated ballerina. In the dark days that followed the Revolution Spessivtseva remained true to her parent theatre at a time when many other ballerinas had quit their native land. She thus inherited many roles – Nikiya in *La Bayadère* and Esmeralda were among her early triumphs – and also assumed a role which became uniquely hers: Giselle. In the part, the mystery of her personality, certain unguessable and untouchable tragic facets of her being, seemed to become focused.

In 1921 she travelled to the West again, to participate in the celebrated Diaghilev staging of *The Sleeping Princess* in London. Diaghilev had chosen to mount this greatest of the Russian classics in order to give himself a breathing space in which to find a new choreographer after the departure of Massine. He also hoped that it would prove a long-running success so that he could recoup his finances. The designs were by Leon Bakst and as many of the finest classic dancers in the old Russian academic style as Diaghilev could find were invited to take part. He entrusted the opening performance of Aurora to Spessivtseva, and two other exceptional ballerinas – Lubov Egorova and Vera Trefilova (whose purity of style earned her the sobriquet of 'the Ingres of the dance') – were lined up to follow her, while Lydia Lopokova and Vera Nemchinova also undertook several performances.

Of Spessivtseva's interpretation few sensible comments remain. The most telling comes from Boris Kochno, Diaghilev's secretary and amanuensis who, in *Diaghilev and the Ballet Russe*, tells of a rehearsal in London with Spessivtseva. 'She began to rehearse Aurora's variation. The others, who were working all over the room, stopped one by one and stood motionless, watching her dance. Smiling, she moved with an

Olga Spessivtseva as Aurora in the Diaghilev Ballet's production of The Sleeping Princess *in London in 1921. Her costume is by Bakst.*

extraordinary serenity and ease, and the virtuoso steps she was executing seemed simple and natural. She never had to reach for a balance; she seemed sustained by an invisible thread. At the end of the variation there was a long and admiring silence and then the room exploded into applause – company rules forbade it but that day it was Diaghilev himself who first gave the signal.'

A similar revelatory rehearsal came three years later when Spessivtseva was engaged to dance Giselle for the first time in the West at the Paris Opéra. Her biographer, André Schaikevich, described how the artists of the Opéra ballet were expecting 'a dazzling stranger, and they saw a thin ghost of a woman, her gaze sad, downcast. Her costume also shocked everyone. Coming into the Rotonde rehearsal room, immediately after having done her own class elsewhere, she had her hair clinging to her cheeks, a thin, pale face, and a modest tutu. On her legs she wore wool coverings, one yellow, the other black. She nodded timidly, and went to the barre. The astonishment, the general disappointment were difficult to describe. People asked themselves if she could even stand upright. A few *dégagés,* a few *frappés,* a *grand battement* and everyone was already conquered, fascinated, amazed. The rehearsal began. At the beginning Spessivtseva only marked the steps, but with the mad scene she started to dance. A miraculous transformation occurred in her. Around her the other dancers, motionless with feeling and admiration, were struck dumb. Several wept. All were overcome. Rehearsing the second act, she revealed the complete security of her technique, the entire polish of her execution, her supremely aristocratic style, her moving dramatic presence and an elevation, an imponderable lightness. She gave herself totally to the dance. Her soul danced and the simplest movement became a miracle of beauty which allowed one no time to consider its virtuosity . . .'

It was Spessivtseva's tragedy that she never found, outside Russia, the setting of a great company – which a classic ballerina needs quite as much as a classic company needs a ballerina – to show off her gifts. Her career, once she finally left Russia in 1923, was itinerant. She appeared as a guest at the Paris Opéra; she danced intermittently with Diaghilev, appeared in Buenos Aires and, very importantly, in London in 1932, when she made guest performances with the Camargo Society at the Savoy Theatre as Giselle and Odette in *Swan Lake* Act II. She also made an Australian tour with the successor to the Pavlova company, the Dandré-Levitov Russian Ballet, during which signs of nervous instability made their distressing first appearance. Returning to Europe, she danced in some performances with her own group, made a last trip to South America, and then settled in the United States. By this time she had virtually given up dancing, and eventually found refuge in a mental institution where she remained for twenty years. In 1963 the intercession of friends and a reassessment of her treatment brought her back into the world, where she lives in quiet retirement in New York State. It must be seen that the greatness of her art has been matched by the greatness of her suffering. A glimpse of her dancing in *Giselle* is preserved on some amateur film made in London. As with the Pavlova fragments, the genius of the artist transcends all the inadequacies of the film.

The Ballets Russes

It is a remarkable fact that the idea of 'Russian' ballet was spread throughout the West by an organisation which never appeared in Russia itself. Diaghilev's early seasons of ballet (and opera) were produced with artists, choreographers and designers who were products of the Russian theatre and theatrical traditions, but the Ballet Russe never performed in Russia, and with the outbreak of the war in 1914, and the subsequent Revolution of 1917, Diaghilev was cut off for ever from Russia. He used only Russian choreographers – Nijinsky briefly succeeded Fokine as creator, to be followed by Massine, Bronislava Nijinska and, finally, in 1924, George Balanchine, who had just arrived from the Soviet Union – but he was forced to recruit dancers in the West (although he turned them, in effect, into Russians by training and by artistic education) and his constant quest for the new in the arts brought early association with European composers, and then designers.

The Ballet Russe de Serge Diaghilev was to find a home in Monte Carlo by 1923 and, after Diaghilev's death in 1929, when his company instantly disbanded, it was Monte Carlo which was to be the launching pad for the revived Ballet Russe de Monte Carlo troupe which emerged in 1932 to assume the mantle of the earlier enterprise and perpetuate the idea of the glamorous and exotic 'Russian' ballet.

The most celebrated of the international star ballerinas of the Ballets Russes, and the most glamorous, was Alexandra Danilova. Born in St Petersburg in 1904, she studied at the Imperial Ballet School in her native city in the extraordinary and disturbed period that bridged the Revolution of 1917, and graduated in 1922, having been taught by some of the most illustrious teachers, including Vaganova, Claudia Kulichevskaya, Julia Siedova and Elizaveta Gerdt, who was still a ballerina of the company. An exceedingly gifted student, Danilova seemed clearly destined for a leading position in the company of the new Soviet State Ballet. But in the summer of 1924 she was part of a group of four young dancers from Leningrad, led by George Balanchine, who set out on a concert tour of the Baltic. They were not to return to their native land: by the autumn of that year they had been recruited by Diaghilev for his Ballet Russe (Balanchine becoming the company's final ballet master) and the course of Danilova's career was set on a new, very different path.

If any one dancer can be said to have enshrined the ideals of the Ballets Russes over the next thirty years, it is Danilova. With Diaghilev she attained ballerina status, and with the emergence of the Ballet Russe de Monte Carlo in the early ·1930s she was recognised as the leading ballerina of the ensemble. Her roles with Diaghilev included those in *Le Bal*, *Ode*, *Swan Lake* Act II, Terpsichore in *Apollo*, and *La Boutique fantasque*, a list which provides some indication of her range, from the soubrette sparkle of her Can Can dancer in *La Boutique fantasque* to the grandeur of her Swan Queen, which she danced with unalterable rightness until her retirement. With the de Basil company (which emerged as the successor to the Ballet Russe after the death of Diaghilev), Danilova confirmed a choreographic and dance partnership with Léonide Massine which had begun with Diaghilev and when, in 1938, Massine split with de Basil and became artistic director of the newly formed Ballet Russe de Monte Carlo, it was inevitable that Danilova should become a leading ballerina with the company. The portraits Massine created for her in *Gaîeté Parisienne* and as the Street Dancer in *Le Beau Danube* were potent images for the Russian ballet. Later, Danilova's partnership with Balanchine was re-established when he revived his version of *Le Baiser de la fée* and created the role of the Somnambulist in *Night Shadow* for her, as well as the ballerina part in *Danses Concertantes*.

But the role that best enshrines the image of Danilova as recognised by her vast and adoring public is that of Swanilda in *Coppélia*. In the part, her classical distinction as a ballerina was perfectly allied to the effervescent charm of her personality – that charm which could galvanise any role and bring it to vivid life in the theatre. The eminent American critic Edwin Denby observed, 'Among ballet stars, Danilova has a special gift. At the height of a classical variation, while she is observing all the restrictions of the grand style, she seems suddenly to be happy to be dancing, with a pleasure like a little girl's. It gives her a sort of natural grace that is unique ... you feel, in the sustained flow of Danilova's rhythm, the alert vivacity of her personal dance imagination, the bite and grace of her feminine temperament and a human sincerity that makes an artist both unpretentious and great.'

In partnership with Frederic Franklin, Danilova long sustained the identity of the Ballet Russe de Monte Carlo, and the many tours during the 1940s and 1950s meant that for thousands of people across the United States Danilova and Franklin were the incarnation of 'ballet' as, in similar circumstances in Britain, were Markova and Dolin. It is this aspect of the ballerina's art, the ability to become the soul of a company and to seem the guardian of its finest qualities, that is so remarkable in Danilova's career. The grandeur of her style and her power to communicate the delight of ballet to her public are among her unique gifts. It is worth noting that her style, formed in the grandest traditions of the Imperial Russian Ballet, remained constant and coherent throughout her long career. When the Kirov Ballet, the successor of the St Petersburg Ballet, made its first Western appearances at Covent Garden in 1961, its dance style for many observers was not altogether unfamiliar: some of its best aspects had been foreshadowed in the performances of Alexandra Danilova in such ballets as *Swan Lake* and *The Nutcracker*.

Although she was born in London in 1910 as Lilian Alicia Marks, making her first appearance as a child dancer in pantomime at the age of ten (when she was billed as 'little Alicia, the child Pavlova'), the 'Russianness' of Alicia Markova's dancing

Above *A publicity photograph of Danilova, taken in the early 1940s, which epitomises the glamour of this great star of the Ballet Russe de Monte Carlo.*

Right *Danilova as Terpsichore in Balanchine's Apollo in its original production for Diaghilev. The tutus of the Muses, designed by Diaghilev's friend Chanel, varied in length, depending upon the quality of the ballerina's legs. Danilova's skirt was the shortest; her legs were the best.*

Previous page *Irina Baronova as the Doll in* Petrushka.

heritage was there from the start. She was a pupil of the distinguished Russian teacher Serafine Astafieva and it was in her studio that Diaghilev saw the prodigious little girl and decided to engage her, despite her extreme youth, for his ballet company. At the age of fourteen, Alicia Marks became Alicia Markova and began the career which has made her a legendary name in the ballet of this century. Her repertory with Diaghilev included the creation of the Nightingale in Balanchine's *Le Rossignol,* and while still a teenager she was entrusted with leading roles which she performed in the greatest theatres of Europe.

During her five years with the Ballet Russe the young dancer came to maturity, but Diaghilev's death in 1929, and the disbanding of his company, seemed to put an end to her career. Markova returned to London, and was soon involved in the earliest stirrings of the infant British ballet. To earn her livelihood she had to dance in cinemas, but she also joined in the performances of the Rambert Ballet Club and the Vic-Wells (now Royal) Ballet, both young troupes that were making the first steps which were to lead to the proper establishment of ballet in Britain.

Ballets were being created for Markova by Frederick Ashton, Antony Tudor and Ninette de Valois, but her exceptional elegance and the distinction of her Russian schooling (she was a pupil of Enrico Cecchetti and of Nikolay Legat, formerly the *premier danseur* of the Maryinsky Theatre) fitted her for the classics of the nineteenth-century Russian repertory that Ninette de Valois acquired in order to give a sound basis to the national ballet she was creating in Britain. Thus, in 1934, Markova justified the staging of *Giselle* (a ballet with which she was to be intimately associated thereafter) as well as *The Nutcracker* and the full-length *Swan Lake*. In these performances her exquisite lightness, the classic purity of her style and her power to draw an audience into the imaginative world of the ballet she was interpreting, were superbly displayed.

In 1935 Markova, with Anton Dolin, the *premier danseur* with whom her name is so closely linked in partnership, formed the Markova-Dolin Ballet, which toured Britain for two years, building a new audience for ballet. Then, for the next ten years, her career was largely spent in America, first with the Ballet Russe de Monte Carlo and then with American Ballet Theatre. Markova was hailed as one of the greatest ballerinas of this century. Her performance as Giselle, technically brilliant with imponderable grace and delicate pathos, probably best represented her art at this time. After returning as guests of the Sadler's Wells Ballet at Covent Garden in 1948, Markova and Dolin were soon to form a new company, Festival Ballet, which toured and played London seasons, reviving some of the most celebrated works of the Ballet Russe era, as well as the classics. In this repertory Markova and Dolin, and such distinguished guests as Alexandra Danilova, Léonide Massine, Yvette Chauviré, Tatiana Riabouchinska, Tamara Toumanova and Mia Slavenska, reasserted the function of the star dancer to stimulate the public by his or her artistry and unique communicative power.

Markova's range was considerable. As Antony Tudor's Juliet (in the *Romeo and Juliet* which he created for her in New York in 1943), in Massine's symphonic ballets,

The very young Irina Baronova (aged 15 years) and the 16-year-old André Eglevsky rehearsing David Lichine's Les Imaginaires *which was shown in London during the summer of 1934. The ballet, which had music by Auric and costumes by Comte Etienne de Beaumont, was about geometrical figures chalked on a blackboard and then erased. The consensus of critical opinion was that the ballet proved nothing.*
Previous page *Alicia Markova and Igor Youskevitch in Massine's* Rouge et Noir, *threatened by the shadow of André Eglevsky. The designs were by Matisse.*

Rouge et Noir and *Seventh Symphony*, as the fiery gypsy in his *Aleko*, and as the reincarnation of Taglioni in Dolin's reconstruction of the *Pas de Quatre*, Markova's purity of technique was allied to an extraordinary precision of physical and dramatic effect.

Edwin Denby provides the most perceptive descriptions of her art, telling how she showed 'the quiet simplicity of a great style, by believing completely in the piece she was performing ... She is a completely objective artist. Who Markova is, nobody knows. What you see on the stage is the piece she performs, the character she acts. She shows you, as only the greatest of actresses do, a completely fascinating impersonation, completely fascinating because you recognise a heroine of the imagination who finds out all about vanity and love and authority and death. You watch her discover them. Markova's Juliet is a miracle of acting. Every nuance of pantomime is poignantly clear and every moment is a different aspect of the cumulative tragedy.'

The three Russian-born 'baby' ballerinas, Irina Baronova, Tatiana Riabouchinska and Tamara Toumanova, came to public fame in 1932 with the establishment by

René Blum of a new Ballet Russe company which assumed the mantle of the émigré Russian ballet after Diaghilev's death. It was George Balanchine, the first choreographer for Blum's Ballet Russe, who recruited these three outstanding young girls from the Paris studios where two of the greatest stars of the Russian Imperial Ballet, Mathilda Kschessinskaya and Olga Preobrazhenskaya, were teaching. All three girls were in their early teens. Irina Baronova, born in Petrograd in 1919 and a pupil of Madame Preo, already had professional dancing experience, as had Tatiana Riabouchinska, who was born in 1917 in Moscow, and was a pupil of Kschessinskaya; while Tamara Toumanova, another Preo pupil, had been born in a train near Shanghai in 1919.

All three girls were preternaturally gifted and proved happily able to take the leading roles which Balanchine created for them in the first season of the company. Their presence might have smacked of cheap publicity – and they were invaluable as box-office draws – but their artistry and exceptional talents are in no doubt. Their youth, their beauty and their extravagant technical ability were to win them the instant fame that can come briefly to young prodigies, but is rarely sustained. However, the career of Alicia Markova (who had joined Diaghilev at the age of fourteen) and of these three wonderful girls are proof that precocious ability can fulfil its early promise.

The Ballet Russe de Monte Carlo was a hard school. The baby ballerinas had to work unceasingly. Despite the difficulties of touring, constant performance and the expectations of a public to whom the words 'Ballet Russe' meant the standards of the Diaghilev troupe, the girls were never pampered and they had to meet every demand made on them by Balanchine and his successor as choreographer, after a year, Léonide Massine. Each girl's style, appearance and manner were refreshingly different from those of her companions. Baronova was the youngest looking, extremely pretty, and her dancing was imbued with an enchanting sense of fun and an uncanny ease. Tamara Toumanova was dark and very beautiful: Arnold Haskell, the English critic who followed their careers, called her 'the black pearl of the Russian ballet'. Like Baronova, she was a phenomenal technician, both girls' skill passed to them by their teacher Preobrazhenskaya, herself one of the great virtuosos of the Imperial Ballet. Riabouchinska, slightly older than the other two, was blonde and blessed with a ravishing lightness of jump and of technical style which her teacher Kschessinskaya had given her. In the taxing world of a touring ballet company, where everything was expected of them, they grew up as dancers and as artists, and the public adulation which surrounded them seems hardly to have touched them. They were protected by their mothers (the image of the 'ballet mother', fighting like a tigress for her child, emerged very strongly if rather unjustly at this time) but the girls were ready to accept the challenges that they set each other. Baronova and Toumanova rejoiced in competitions at turning *fouettés,* delighting in performing steps that defeated many another ballerina with young girls' pleasure in showing off their physical facility.

That this extraordinary trio were not mechanically able but unthinking infant prodigies is testified by the roles that were created for them, by the respect afforded them by critics, and by the adoration of the public which lasted throughout their careers. Very significantly they were able, as they reached maturity, to enhance many of the traditional roles of the repertory, especially Baronova and Toumanova, as they were more conventional ballerina material. Riabouchinska was unsurpassed in certain ballets on which she set an indelible stamp: the Prelude in *Les Sylphides*; the Florentine Girl in Fokine's *Paganini*; the Golden Cockerel in *Le Coq d'Or*; and Princess Florine in the Blue Bird *pas de deux*, as well as several roles created for her by Massine.

Toumanova was given memorable roles by Balanchine very early on, notably in *Le Cotillon*, and then, when she joined him for his short-lived Les Ballets 1933, in *Mozartiana* and *Les Songes*. She also shone in Massine's *Jardin Public* and exceptionally in his *Symphonie fantastique* of 1936. Baronova sparkled in Massine's *Jeux d'Enfants* and in *Le Beau Danube*, in the tiny role of the First Hand, and in the first of his symphonic ballets, *Les Présages* in 1933, and in Bronislava Nijinska's *Les Cent Baisers*. The repertory of Baronova and Toumanova was in many ways alike, for both were able to dance the nineteenth-century classics in the one-act versions then being toured by the Ballet Russe – appearing as Aurora in *Aurora's Wedding* and Odette in *Swan Lake* Act II.

The vicissitudes of the Ballet Russe were to bring a separation of these three box-office draws. When Colonel de Basil, who had gained control of the Ballet Russe, and Léonide Massine, its choreographer and star dancer, parted, there came a series of bewildering changes of company name and personnel in the late 1930s which led Riabouchinska and Baronova to stay for a time with Colonel de Basil, while Toumanova went to join Massine's new Ballet Russe de Monte Carlo. In the sensational summer of 1938 ballet fans in London were able to shuttle between Covent Garden and the Theatre Royal, Drury Lane, avidly following the rival repertories and the rival stars of the two Ballet Russe ensembles. This sort of glamour and excitement is unknown today, although it has been possible in New York during the spring season on Lincoln Center Plaza to move between performances of New York City Ballet and American Ballet Theatre, dashing to see Suzanne Farrell in one ballet in one theatre and then crossing the plaza to catch Natalia Makarova in another theatre and another ballet.

As the baby ballerinas grew up and went their separate ways, their careers altered. In a most perceptive assessment in her book on the de Basil company, the distinguished critic Kathrine Sorley Walker discusses the careers and artistry of these three exceptional young women. She makes the excellent point that their greatest and most influential years were inevitably during the decade of the 1930s and that 'By the time they were in their early twenties they were veterans. Their mental attitude to ballet had altered and they were looking outside the world they had grown up in for new artistic and emotional experiences.'

Baronova made two films and joined American Ballet Theatre at its inception,

Tamara Toumanova in the second act of
Coppélia. *This Hollywood photograph conveys*
a great deal of the beauty and allure of the black
pearl of the Russian ballet.

where she danced throughout the early 1940s before her retirement in 1946, leaving the stage for marriage and motherhood. In recent years she has returned to give master classes and to coaching, in which she demonstrates a style of exceptional nobility and grace. Tatiana Riabouchinska stayed with the de Basil company with her husband, David Lichine, returning to London in 1947 with the troupe, and then made guest appearances with the Grand Ballet du Marquis de Cuevas, with Festival Ballet and with the Ballets des Champs-Elysées. Toumanova also appeared in films and made many guest appearances, dancing with Festival Ballet, the Paris Opéra Ballet (where she created the role of Phèdre in the ballet by Lifar and Cocteau) and with the Grand Ballet du Marquis de Cuevas, as well as giving dance recitals. Her power and the glamour of her presence often illuminated indifferent works, as was evident in her galvanising of an otherwise flaccid *Esmeralda* for Festival Ballet.

Tatiana Riabouchinska in one of her most celebrated roles, the Prelude in Les Sylphides. *The lightness of her style and her withdrawn beauty in this famous solo have seldom been surpassed.*

Ballerinas of the Soviet Union

Looking back on the history of dance, it is possible to distinguish certain ballerinas whose particular genius has changed the nature of ballet, bringing new audiences and a new energy to the art. It may be that their physical prowess or their style of dancing has broken the dance-mould of the past; they may have stressed some aspect of the art which has hitherto been neglected. Such, as we have seen, was the case with Marie Taglioni, whose Sylphide banished the old style of ballet from the stage of the Paris Opéra. Virginia Zucchi's performances in St Petersburg in the 1880s caught the imagination of dancers and public alike so that a new appreciation of ballet was born in Russia, and by stimulating Alexandre Benois's love of dance she had an indirect but appreciable influence upon the emergence of the Ballets Russes. Other ballerinas at different times – Pavlova, Markova – have left an unmistakable mark on the history of ballet. In Soviet Russia, the début of Marina Semyonova played a crucial part in helping to secure ballet's existence during the difficult post-Revolutionary years. As with so much in Russian life, the identity of ballet itself was called into question in these troubled times. There were attacks by doctrinaire Marxist theorists eager to reject the greatness of Russian ballet as developed under Tsarist patronage. They wanted to substitute an art, said the choreographer Leonid Yakobson, 'taking themes from surrounding Soviet reality, resolving class-proletarian problems, exciting and activising, breaking with the rule-encircled and helpless dance of the past and by every means trying to create a theatre of the great proletarian culture'. In opposition to this view were such figures as the Commissar for Education, Anatoly Lunarcharsky, and the ballerina Agrippina Vaganova, whose teaching was to form the basis of the new Soviet dance style. A distinguished soloist, and then a ballerina, at the Mariinsky Theatre, she had retired in 1916 to teach, and her classes in Petrograd from 1920 were to be the proving ground of a new and vital extension of the old Imperial Ballet manner which – without destroying the dignity and elegance of the Russian school – strengthened and extended it for the new society in which ballet was to have to work. Vaganova set about analysing the teaching methods of such masters as Enrico Cecchetti and the celebrated Imperial ballerina Olga Preobrazhenskaya. Her system was thereafter to produce the first astounding generations of Soviet ballerinas, headed by Marina Semyonova and followed by Galina Ulanova, Natalia Dudinskaya, Alla Shelest, Tatiana Vecheslova and, finally, her last pupil, Irina Kolpakova. In 1934 she became director of the Kirov Theatre Ballet in Leningrad, the new name given to the former Mariinsky Theatre Ballet in St Petersburg.

The desire to preserve, to explore and to enhance ballet for the Soviet audience, an ideal which inspired Vaganova as it did Lunarcharsky, received a tremendous boost with the début of Marina Semyonova, who was the first and arguably the greatest of Vaganova's many pupils. Born in 1908 in St Petersburg, she began her studies with Vaganova in 1919 and graduated into the Leningrad company in 1925. Her graduation performance was made in Vaganova's restaging of *La Source*, a ballet in which Vaganova herself had appeared with great success in her time. Vaganova composed new variations for her pupil, allowing Semyonova to display her magnificent *plastique,* her astounding 'impetuous' leaps and her impeccable *pointe* work. A Soviet critic noted: 'Her appearance made possible the rousing of a dying trend. The drowning grasp at her as at a straw. They strive to turn a postponement into a salvation.' That her appearance was to have a permanent effect upon the future of Soviet Ballet is in no doubt. Her dancing spoke directly to the public, and to the

Left *Agrippina Vaganova as Odette in the second act of* Swan Lake *at the Mariinsky Theatre.*
Below *Marina Semyonova as Pannochka in* Taras Bulba.
Previous page *Olga Preobrazhenskaya: a rare back-stage photograph taken in 1910.*

critics of ballet, of the life-asserting splendour of the classic dance and of its possibilities in a new society. The Soviet historian Natalia Roslavleva observed: 'Semyonova's début in the former Mariinsky Theatre ... was in a ballerina role, that of Aurora in *The Sleeping Beauty*. Technically she was superb, but it was the life-asserting quality of her dancing that inspired the audience with a feeling of exhilaration.'

It was the ability to hold her audience by the physical grandeur and emotional drive of her dancing which marked Semyonova's entire career. Associated particularly with the classic repertory, her Aurora, Odette-Odile in *Swan Lake*, Raymonda and Nikiya in *La Bayadère* were ideal examples of how the Soviet ballerina might interpret these roles for a new audience and a new world. Throughout the 1930s and 1940s, when she had transferred to the Moscow Bolshoi Theatre as its *assoluta*, Semyonova's art was a beacon for lovers of the classic dance. She retired in 1954, and since that time she has devoted herself to teaching, giving a *classe de perfection* at the Bolshoi and coaching. In this way she had passed on the heritage learned from Vaganova, enriched with her own experience, to such pupils as Plisetskaya, Makarova, Semenyaka and many others, ensuring that Soviet ballerinas take the stage armed with the performing wisdom and artistic sensibility of many generations, garnered and treasured from ballerina teacher to ballerina pupil, from Vazem to Vaganova, from Vaganova to Semyonova, from Semyonova to the ballerinas of today – a long chain of experience stretching back over a century. Throughout their careers they further explore and embellish the interpretation of the major roles with their own artistry, and every difficulty they conquer, each new nuance of interpretation they add, becomes part of a treasure house of received learning which will in time be passed on to the next generation of ballerinas. To ignore this method of forming artists, as ballet companies such as the Royal Ballet do at their peril, is to condemn future ballerinas to a perpetual struggle to reach the peaks achieved by their predecessors, rather than moving on, as in Russia, from that peak to further and grander achievement.

If any one dancer typifies for Western audiences the artistry of Soviet ballet, it is Galina Ulanova. She made her Western début initially in Italy in a concert performance, and then, in 1956, in a proper setting, with the full panoply of the Bolshoi Ballet when the company made its first, astounding appearances at Covent Garden. By that time, for long a legendary name, Ulanova was in the final years of her career as a ballerina, but the special communicative magic of her interpretations was exceptionally potent. She conquered London and, three years later, at the age of forty-nine, New York.

What had gripped the imagination of Western audiences, as it had previously the Russian public, was an apparent modesty of manner and an interpretation which scaled extraordinary heights of lyricism. Her Giselle, happily preserved on film in performance with the Bolshoi at Covent Garden in 1956, is a portrait of rare quietness, with a sense of humanity that infuses the Romantic drama with new and touching life. It was an interpretation in which, as one Russian critic noted, 'Every movement is wholly justified, it is a clear language of mime and of dance. Her simplest movements contain the most delicate meaning ... all seems simple and perfectly clear.' Her lyricism, according to another Soviet writer, 'is deeply national, truly Russian. It is a lyricism that displays miracles of fortitude and courage, the lyricism of a heart that suffers heroically. Her art is an art that reaches out for a definite goal, it is attuned to the times and being the art of a genuinely modest artist is directed to the future.' In these observations we can sense the way in which Ulanova's artistry has, for the public both inside the Soviet Union and outside that country, seemed the embodiment of a central fact about Soviet ballet and its aims in portraying the strivings of humanity.

Ulanova was the daughter of two dancers in St Petersburg, where she was born in 1910, and was a pupil first of her mother, Maria Romanova, then of Vaganova,

Right Galina Ulanova as Maria and Vladimir Bakanov as Khan Girei in Rostislav Zakharov's The Fountain of Bakchisaray *at the Bolshoi Theatre. The ballet is based on Pushkin's poem of the same name. Maria, a Polish princess, is abducted by the Khan but rejects his love. However, she has aroused the jealousy of his mistress Zarema, who finally stabs her. As the chaste and sorrowing Maria, Ulanova had one of her most moving and eloquent roles.*
Far right Galina Ulanova coaching one of the new generation of Bolshoi stars, Alla Mikhalchenko, in Raymonda *during the Bolshoi Ballet's visit to London in 1986.*

in whose classes her contemporary was to be another great Soviet ballerina. Very different from Ulanova in her technique and force of personality, Tatiana Vecheslova was to star for many years with the Leningrad Ballet. Ulanova graduated in 1928, and it was soon obvious that in her dancing Soviet ballet had found a key image.

'Her art speaks to the mind and moves the heart,' it was said, and Ulanova, with her sensitivity of style, was to become the favoured muse of several choreographers during the 1930s and 1940s, when Soviet ballet was itself finding its identity. Thus, even during the early years of her career, when she was learning her interpretative craft in the traditional classics, Ulanova was already creating major roles in the new repertory: in Vainonen's *The Flames of Paris* in 1932, which dealt with the French Revolution; in Zakharov's *The Fountain of Bakchisaray* of 1934, adapted from a Pushkin poem; and in his *Lost Illusions* of 1936, after Balzac; and, most remarkably,

in Lavrovsky's *Romeo and Juliet* of 1940. In all these ballets, produced in Leningrad where her career flowered, Ulanova laid claim to a dominant position in the realisation of an ideal heroine for Russian ballet. In 1944 she joined the Moscow Bolshoi Ballet where, in 1945, she created the part of Cinderella in Zakharov's new production, and also assumed the leading role of Parasha in his *The Bronze Horseman* and the role of the heroine Toa Hua in Lavrovsky's version of the revolutionary ballet *The Red Poppy* in 1949.

In the Soviet Union Ulanova is revered as a ballerina whose intensity of characterisation is laden with truth and meaning. 'To Ulanova the technique of the classic dance is the means for creating a portrait and embodying an idea. Moreover, her technique always suggests to her the simplest and most direct medium for expressing the emotions of her heroine. Her dance is neither dazzling nor stunning but there is in it a comforting luminousness and a natural grace ... She wants to show people not as they are but as they should be. By sublimating her heroines she, as it were, upholds the eternal humanitarian ideals' (V. Bogdanov Beresovsky).

It was this heartfelt aspiration, the sensitivity and gentle strength of Ulanova's manner and of her dance characterisations, which struck so strong an emotive chord in her public. Her suffering but nobly pure Giselle, and her aspiring Juliet, marked at every moment by a moral integrity, were for Russian ballet central cultural facts which could be set against the grandeur of Semyonova, and the astounding virtuosity of Natalia Dudinskaya, or the explosive technical brilliance and emotional bravura of Plisetskaya. It was Ulanova's ability to broadcast feeling, to fill out the characters she danced with her own special feminine dignity and grace, which won her universal admiration. She retired from the stage in 1962 and has since then coached and rehearsed many younger ballerinas, including Yekaterina Maximova and Nadezhda Pavlova.

There could be no greater contrast with the almost contemplative quietness of Ulanova's manner than the interpretations of another, outstanding Soviet ballerina: Natalia Dudinskaya. She was the possessor of an astounding technique which, unlike the virtuosity of certain other brilliant dancers, was controlled by the canons of strictest academic form. Her every feat of bravura dancing attained an ideal of classical purity which marked her as a dancer of magnificent talent. There is a brief film showing Dudinskaya with Vakhtang Chabukiany, a blazing virtuoso of the Kirov Ballet and her frequent partner, in the Shades scene from *La Bayadère* which conveys something of the amazing skill and classic rigour of her style in one of the supreme passages of academic dancing. It was Dudinskaya's astonishing virtuosity which inspired Chabukiany to create for her the leading role of Laurencia in his ballet of that name in Leningrad in 1939.

Dudinskaya was born in Kharkov in 1912. Like Ulanova, she was initially taught by her mother, then entered Vaganova's classes at the Leningrad Ballet School. She graduated in 1931 into the Kirov Ballet and was marked for early stardom: her first full-length *Swan Lake* came within six months of her début with the company.

Thereafter she was to perform much of the company repertory, and in the post-war years she was to create leading roles in ballets produced by her husband, Konstantin Sergeyev; notably his *Cinderella* in 1946 and his dramatic ballet about apartheid in South Africa, *The Path of Thunder,* in 1957.

Dudinskaya, alas, was never to dance in the West, although it is worth recording that a petition was handed to the directorate of the Kirov Ballet at the time of the company's first visit to London in 1961 requesting that Dudinskaya and Sergeyev, then in charge of the troupe, might be seen in performance. Her career in Russia brought her tremendous acclaim as an exponent of the most dazzling virtuosity, and she has also gained a great reputation as a teacher. She has, since her retirement from dancing, taught the *classe de perfection* at the Kirov Ballet, passing on the priceless heritage of her own career and her Vaganova training to her pupils, one of whom was Natalia Makarova (who also studied with Tatiana Vecheslova and Alla Shelest). Makarova, in her *Dance Autobiography,* writes that Dudinskaya's teaching developed stamina and technical skill by 'driving and urging me on unmercifully in the classroom. She possessed such will, and such uncontradictable authority, that I did not dare, for instance, to break off a variation being rehearsed, however exhausted or tense I might be. I did not dare not finish something. "Don't stop, keep going," she would demand like a sergeant-major ... Dancers can't be self-pitying – they must have a masochism of the ballet in their blood or they will never realise their potential ... to triumph over the body, to cultivate this balletic masochism – this Dudinskaya taught me.'

This dedication is a lesson that every ballerina learns and, as performer, as teacher and as pupil, it is central to the attaining of that physical command which frees the spirit and the body to dance. Of Dudinskaya as a performer, Makarova notes: 'She had been brilliantly schooled by Vaganova and possessed phenomenal technique – a fabulous soaring jump and all kinds of *tours* – as well as the most appealing dance energy. Even at fifty-seven she could perform double *tours* on the diagonal, crossing the Kirov stage at enormous speed. No wonder she was acclaimed as a real virtuoso, trained in the best traditions of the former Maryinsky ... her technique remained unmatchable through her final performances on the Kirov stage.'

A comparable virtuoso from the Moscow School was Olga Lepeshinskaya, who graduated into the Bolshoi Ballet in 1933 at the age of seventeen. She was at once recognised as a ballerina, a tribute to the vitality and brilliance of her physical skills. A small figure of extrovert personality, she excelled in roles which demanded a *demi-caractère* charm and the extravagant prowess she could so effortlessly deploy. As Kitri in *Don Quixote,* as Lise in the Russian version of *La Fille mal gardée* and as Cinderella in Zakharov's staging at the Bolshoi, she was seen at her very best. So she was in her one major Western appearance with the Bolshoi Ballet in Paris in 1962, as the heroine of Vainonen's *Mirandolina*. In this adaptation of a Goldoni comedy, Lepeshinskaya offered such prodigies of skill, and displayed such tireless and effervescent dancing, that she seemed to blaze with light. Her virtuosity was an astonishment, and it was easy to comprehend how she had conquered a vast public in Russia by her ebullient charm and the fireworks of her technique. Since retirement Lepeshinskaya has been much sought after as a teacher and emissary of Soviet training to ballet companies in both Western and Eastern blocs.

In the art of Maya Plisetskaya we are confronted with the quintessential Moscow ballerina, powerful in emotional projection, thrilling in technique, showing in everything a fire of temperament. She was marked out for the theatre: her uncle and aunt, Asaf and Sulamith Messerer, were leading dancers of the Bolshoi Ballet; her mother was an actress; her cousin a designer; one of her brothers, Azary, has also been a dancer; and she possesses a magnificent natural physique for dancing, with her beautiful head poised on a long neck and her long limbs which have the flexibility and power to draw unforgettable choreographic images. She was trained at the Moscow Ballet School and was a pupil of Elizaveta Gerdt, an eminent ballerina whose career from 1908–28 spanned the years of great change in Russian ballet, and who subsequently became a most influential teacher, even, briefly, of Vaganova. Graduating into the Bolshoi Ballet in 1943 at the age of seventeen, Plisetskaya was to study further with her uncle and aunt, and with Marina Semyonova.

Above *Natalia Dudinskaya teaching in the Leningrad school.*

Previous page *Dudinskaya and Konstantin Sergeyev in Zakharov's* The Bronze Horseman.

Right *Olga
Lepeshinskaya with
attendant fauns in the
Walpurgisnacht
divertissement from
Gounod's* Faust *as staged
by the Bolshoi Ballet.*
Far right *Maya
Plisetskaya, heroic as the
Dying Swan.*

Plisetskaya, her prodigious physical instrument tuned by her ballerina teachers, was soon to claim major roles for her own, notably Odette-Odile in *Swan Lake*, which she first danced in the late 1940s. The magnificent curves of her limbs and back, the proud force of her stance and the irresistible bravura of her Odile were to remain a constant throughout the years that she danced this ballet. Her Swan Queen, proud and challenging, was very different from the grieving Odette proposed by other ballerinas. There was in it, as in all her roles, an undaunted spirit that dominated the stage, the choreography and the audience. In lightweight roles, such as the Tsar Maiden in *The Little Humpbacked Horse*, and especially as Kitri in *Don Quixote,* she was bewitching. Her Kitri, with extravagant jumps, heel touching the back of her head in *grand jeté*, her body curved in splendid arcs and rattling off variations with fan or castanets or tambourine, was a portrait drawn in Spanish sunshine. Her Juliet was noble in outline as in feeling, proud and passionate and wilful; so was her Carmen in an otherwise vapid exercise which she made splendid by her force of temperament. As Phrygia, in a fragment from Yakobson's version of *Spartacus*, the beauty of her *plastique,* the curve of a sandalled foot and the yielding outlines of her back as she dressed Spartacus for battle, were the creations of a supreme sculptor.

In everything Plisetskaya's art demands attention, in its tempestuous force as much as in its indomitable will. She has turned choreographer, staging *Anna Karenina* and *The Seagull* at the Bolshoi, and finding in these ballets roles to fit her artistry in its autumn splendour. She has also worked with Western companies and choreographers, appearing with Maurice Béjart's Ballet of the XXth Century to dance his Leda and also performing his *Isadora,* and dancing with Roland Petit's Ballet de Marseille in *La Rose Malade*, which was created for her. She has lately been seen in a work inspired by the Chekhov short story *The Lady with the Little Dog*, and has danced with the Ballet-Théâtre Français in Lifar's *Phèdre*, in which the blazing passion of her body and her hieratic dignity suggested all the tragedy of the doomed heroine. Her beauty and her stage power are undefeated by the years and she remains the last of the great *monstres sacrés* of ballet.

Alla Shelest demands to be ranked next to Dudinskaya, Lepeshinskaya and Plisetskaya in this survey of Soviet ballerinas. Although she made only one brief visit to the West when she was seen, unforgettably, in a couple of concert performances in London, it was obvious that she possessed exceptional gifts, both as dancer and as dramatic artist. The extent and grandeur of Shelest's art, however, were only properly known by the Leningrad audience who saw the span of her career, and her reputation has hardly reached outside the Soviet Union.

Born in 1919 in Smolensk, Alla Shelest was a pupil of Elizaveta Gerdt and then of Vaganova, and entered the Kirov Ballet in 1937. For the next twenty-five years she combined virtuoso dancing with the emotional intensity of a tragedienne. Accounts of her dancing are not copious, but her reputation is everywhere surrounded by such respect for her gifts and the significance of her contribution to the Leningrad Ballet (for which she created only one major role, that of Aegina in Leonid Yakobson's version of *Spartacus*), that she should not be overlooked. On her retirement she became a teacher in Leningrad, and one of her pupils, Natalia Makarova, writes of the problems of working with this great artist, of the 'tremendous personality' with which she had difficulty in relating, and of Shelest's analytical approach in passing on her insights which did not appear sympathetic to a young artist of the inspirational temperament of Makarova.

As a tribute to Shelest, however, Makarova notes that she retains at least one aspect of her interpretation of Giselle's madness. When, in the mad scene, Giselle recalls dancing with Albrecht, Makarova, like Shelest, performs the steps off the beat and

Two contrasting photographs of Alla Shelest as Jacinta in Vakhtang Chabukiany's staging of Laurencia *for the Kirov Ballet.*

'beyond' the music – the effect of dislocation and tragic breakdown being a souvenir of the art of the great ballerina who was her teacher.

If any ballerina in recent years can be said to represent the purest academic style, it is Irina Kolpakova, the last pupil of Vaganova still to be performing on the ballet stage in 1986. Born in Leningrad in 1933, Kolpakova entered the Ballet School in her native city and, after a period of study with Vaganova, graduated into the ballet of the Kirov Theatre in 1951, the year in which her illustrious teacher died. By means of her temperament, technique, physique and training, Kolpakova was destined to present the classics of the nineteenth century in their most crystalline form, as was shown when she performed her greatest role, Aurora in *The Sleeping Beauty,* on the Kirov Ballet's first visit to London in 1961. Her interpretation was transparently pure and airy, with an especial stylistic radiance. Her exceptional portrayal of this role has happily been preserved on film and, although Kolpakova was in her fiftieth year when it was recorded, it may be seen as a definitive statement of the elegance and rigorous deployment of the classic academic manner as it is understood in Soviet Russia. The youthful charm that Kolpakova showed in her early performances is replaced in this film by a phenomenal clarity and an understanding of the beautiful inevitability of Petipa's choreography. Classical academic dancing could ask for no better statement.

Kolpakova has also been seen in *Raymonda* (an interpretation which has also been filmed), in *Swan Lake, The Nutcracker,* in *La Bayadère* as Nikiya, *La Sylphide* and in *Chopiniana.* In all these roles her almost translucent style seems inevitable. She has an amazingly light technique and the flawlessness of her dancing, combined with her serene, blonde beauty, makes an unforgettable impression. Kolpakova at her greatest seems to have passed beyond technique to the pure source of the classic dance.

Among other Leningrad ballerinas of this era who should be mentioned is Alla Osipenko, another pupil of Vaganova, whose sinuously beautiful line and intensity of presence were admired in *Swan Lake* and superbly used by Yuri Grigorovich in his first major ballet, *The Stone Flower* of 1957, in which Osipenko created the role of the Queen of the Copper Mountain. When the ballet was shown in London on the opening night of the Kirov Ballet's first visit, the role of the heroine Katerina was taken by Alla Sizova, a radiantly gifted dancer of the same generation as Natalia Makarova. Sizova's Aurora has been preserved on film; her gentle dramatic presence and her beautiful jump and *ballon* have illuminated many other ballets in the Kirov repertory. Of the latest generation of Kirov ballerinas, Olga Chenchikova is especially notable as a dazzling and sunny virtuoso, exceptionally remarkable in the bravura showpiece of the *Grand Pas* from *Paquita.* But it is the Moscow generation of Natalia Bessmertnova and Yekaterina Maximova, also contemporaries of Makarova and Sizova, which has had the profoundest influence upon Soviet ballet during the past twenty-five years.

In 1963, on the occasion of the Bolshoi Ballet's second visit to Covent Garden, the ballet critic of the *Financial Times* wrote of Asaf Messerer's *School of Ballet,* a showcase

for the dancers' virtuosity: 'There is one dancer who stands out in this work as she has in every ballet in which she has appeared. On the first night of the season it was obvious that among the three leading swans in *Swan Lake* there was a performer of unique quality, and throughout the season our eyes have been drawn to the slender Natalia Bessmertnova by virtue of her extraordinary grace. I have never before felt so surely that I was watching greatness in a dancer; Miss Bessmertnova has a magical quality that singles her out from every other performer, a mixture of intensity of feeling and effortless projection of dance ideas. Dark-haired, huge-eyed, with long limbs and a supple torso, she is a perfect dance instrument ... She is obviously born to dance Giselle and to assume the great classic roles and revivify them with her magnificent gifts.' These words were written within two years of Bessmertnova's graduation from the Bolshoi Ballet School and these early performances – notably as the Autumn Fairy in *Cinderella* – still linger clearly in the memory.

Bessmertnova did indeed dance Giselle later that same year, making her début in the role she was to enhance throughout her career. Her Giselle was a figure of most

Left *Kolpakova as Aurora in* The Sleeping Beauty *with the Kirov Ballet in London.*
Above *Natalia Bessmertnova as Anastasia and Irek*

Mukhadmedov as Tsar Ivan in Yuri Grigorovich's Ivan the Terrible *as presented by the Bolshoi Ballet at the Royal Opera House, Covent Garden in 1986.*

delicate feeling in the first act, who became the most impalpable of wraiths in the second, in which her lightness and the broad span of her jumps were much to be admired. In time she has inherited all the classic roles. Her husband, Yuri Grigorovich, has been director and chief choreographer for the Bolshoi Ballet since 1964 and Bessmertnova's Odette-Odile in the Grigorovich *Swan Lake* offered an extraordinary combination of elegiac feeling for the Swan Queen and irresistible power for the enchantress. It is in Grigorovich's large-scale ballets for his company, however, that certain aspects of Bessmertnova's art have appeared at their most compelling. As the tragic Anastasia in *Ivan the Terrible* she has created a character of mysterious beauty, the one consolatory point in the Tsar's terrifying story. Best of all, in Grigorovich's recent *The Golden Age* Bessmertnova has given a fascinating double portrait of the heroine, Rita, first as the lyrical girl whose beauty inspires the hero, Boris, to love her and to seek to rescue her from a tawdry life; and as the cabaret dancer whose partnership with the dashing villain, Yashka, shows her in acrobatic and passionate duets in contrast with the two exquisite *pas de deux* which tell of the love of Rita and Boris. Bessmertnova manifests here a vitality and an emotional vivacity to set against the tragic heroines she assumes in the repertory.

If one role typifies the art of Yekaterina Maximova, it is Kitri in *Don Quixote,* a ballet she first danced in 1965 when she was twenty-six and which she instantly claimed as her own. Her youthful prettiness, the sparkle of her dancing and the polished sweetness of her manner allied to what seemed an inextinguishable sense of fun exactly suited Kitri. The role provided a perfect vehicle for Maximova's gifts, especially in partnership with her husband Vladimir Vasiliev, whose technique and sense of humour matched hers. Unlike Plisetskaya, whose performance was a powerful explosion of personality and bravura, Maximova made Kitri seem somehow real and beguiling, a happy girl showing off and fighting for the man she loves, the irresistible Vasiliev.

Maximova was a pupil of Elizaveta Gerdt, and her beautifully rounded technique was seen at its best when she created the role of Masha, the heroine of Grigorovich's *The Nutcracker*. Her childlike innocence and pretty dancing gave the character a touch of wonder that was exactly right for the ballet, while in Grigorovich's monumental staging of *Spartacus* Maximova made Phrygia a vulnerable and heart-rending heroine as she suffered and grieved with Vasiliev's astounding Spartacus.

When Maximova was chosen to dance Giselle she was prepared for her début over a considerable period of time by none other than Galina Ulanova, whose own interpretation had brought a new sense of humanity to the role. It is thus that a continuity of interpretation and technical understanding is guaranteed in Soviet ballet.

From among the present richness of ballerinas in Soviet Russia one further ballerina, Ludmila Semenyaka, must be singled out. A graduate of the Vaganova School in her native Leningrad, where she was born in 1952, she entered the Kirov Ballet in 1969 and within two years she had transferred to the Moscow Bolshoi Ballet where she is now a leading ballerina.

Yekaterina Maximova, irresistibly joyous as Kitri
in Don Quixote *with the Bolshoi Ballet.*

The transfer of artists from Leningrad to Moscow was a regular practice during the 1930s and 1940s, at a time when it was necessary to increase the forces of the Bolshoi Ballet. Traditionally, in Tsarist Russia, the ballet in St Petersburg had always known the lion's share of imperial patronage. Located in the capital city, it was the direct recipient of court attention, and its classic attitudes, aristocratic and eschewing emotionalism, were those of a company which reflected the manners of the court itself. Very different were the traditions of the Moscow Ballet, which had from its inception in the latter years of the eighteenth century always provided its audience

Ludmila Semenyaka and Irek Mukhamedov in the
pas de deux *from Petipa's* Le Talisman *during the*
Bolshoi Ballet's London season in 1986.

with an art that had in it a vivid streak of dramatic temperament. The Moscow public, largely made up of a wealthy merchant class, expected ballet to tell a story in the liveliest terms. Remote from the Tsar's court at St Petersburg, the Moscow Ballet was starved of patronage and of imperial interest. To the ballet world of St Petersburg the art of dancing in Moscow looked extravagant and even vulgar; and there grew up during the nineteenth century a dismissive view of the Moscow troupe. With the Revolution, and the transfer of government to Moscow, ballet in the new capital city was to receive much closer attention. The unifying example of Vaganova's schooling has done much to refine the former extravagances of the Moscow manner, and the Leningrad artists who have been absorbed into the Moscow company during the past half century, from Semyonova, Ulanova and Lavrovsky to Grigorovich and Semenyaka, have helped to change the Bolshoi's attitudes while they have worked to create its present greatness.

Semenyaka's dancing with the Bolshoi Ballet shows a classic authority of especial distinction and charm. She interprets many of the classic and modern roles in the repertory, but it is in *The Sleeping Beauty* and in *Raymonda* that the dignity and grace of her artistry can be most clearly appreciated. Her portrait of Aurora is youthfully delightful but elegant, warm with emotion but controlled and ennobled by the canons of classic style and, as so often is the case with Leningrad-trained dancers, is beautifully light. Watching Semenyaka's Aurora and Raymonda, we understand why Petipa's choreography is great and why it is still vital for ballet in our time. In a role as different as Masha in Grigorovich's *The Nutcracker*, Semenyaka makes no less an enchanting effect. In the hallowed *Dying Swan*, for ever associated with Pavlova but a constant challenge to later ballerinas who have sought to assume her mantle, Semenyaka's simplicity of style and her lyricism make this brief dance poem an episode of rare and lovely emotion.

The Paris Opéra

At the Paris Opéra, after the turn of the century, the Italian manner of bravura performance remained dominant, thanks to the succession of virtuoso *étoiles* trained in Milan, while the repertory declined further and further into facile creations and predictable displays of charm. Carlotta Zambelli and Aida Boni (both Milanese-trained), and later the French *étoiles* Camille Bos and Suzanne Lorcia, took the leading ballerina roles, but this was the the period of Diaghilev and the glamour of the Ballet Russe put activities at the Opéra entirely in the shade.

It was only after Diaghilev's death, when Serge Lifar (the last male star of the Ballet Russe) was invited to become *premier danseur* and *maître de ballet,* that the Opéra was brought back to life. Lifar sought to establish the importance of French ballerinas once more, and although he invited both Marina Semyonova and Olga Spessivtseva to dance at the Opéra, it was with his encouragement that such significant artists as Lucienne Lamballe, Solange Schwarz, Suzanne Lorcia and Lycette Darsonval were brought to prominence. Then, in the late 1930s, a young dancer of marvellous gifts emerged, destined to become a star of the company.

Yvette Chauviré had graduated from the Opéra school into the company in 1935. A pupil of Zambelli, she was later to be much influenced by the teachings of the celebrated Russian instructor in Paris, Boris Kniasev, who opened out her style and polished the essential classicism which was thereafter to mark her as one of the greatest dancers of the century, an artist whom French critics called *La Chauviré Nationale*.

In 1941 she gained the official ranking of *étoile* when she created the leading role in Lifar's *Istar,* and she remained for many years the muse of Lifar at the Opéra, creating roles in twenty of his ballets, notably in *Le Chevalier et la Demoiselle* (1941), *Suite en Blanc* (1943) and *Les Mirages* (1944). In the traditional repertory she made a superlative début in *The Sleeping Beauty* with the Royal Ballet in London in 1958, in which the clarity of her technique was grandly displayed, as was an elegant femininity which spoke so strongly of her native city. But it was as Giselle that she was recognised in every theatre in which she danced as an extraordinarily communicative artist, the delicacy of her dramatic playing being matched by its intensity of feeling and the exquisite purity of her dancing. Since her retirement in 1972, Yvette Chauviré has passed on her knowledge of the great roles by coaching, and has been seen back on stage in the mime role of the Countess in the Opéra staging of *Raymonda*.

Nina Vyroubova was one of two contemporaries of Yvette Chauviré who also contributed to the national and international distinction of French ballet. She was born in Gurzuf in the Crimea in 1921, but arrived in France as a child of three with her mother, who was a dancer and her first teacher. Entrusted thereafter to some of the most important Russian émigrée ballerinas in Paris – Vera Trefilova, Olga Preobrazhenskaya and Lubov Egorova – she made her début at the age of sixteen with a Russian opera company in France. It was as the war ended, and Roland Petit's Ballets des Champs-Elysées were formed, that Vyroubova's career blossomed with the creation of *Les Forains,* in which she danced the role of the Sleeping Beauty, and with a re-staging of Taglioni's *La Sylphide* by Victor Gsovsky, in which she was unforgettably and exquisitely the Sylphide. Possessed of a luminous classic style, she also had that rare gift of seeming to be the incarnation of a poetic ideal, and it is this which made her Sylphide so beautiful and which marked every role she was to dance thereafter.

In 1949 Vyroubova was invited by Serge Lifar to join the Paris Opéra as *étoile,* and during the next seven years she interpreted several important roles that Lifar created for her, in *Les Fourberies de Scapin* and in *The Firebird,* while also taking on much of the traditional Opéra repertory. From 1957 until the dissolution of the company in 1962, Vyroubova was to be the leading ballerina, with Rosella Hightower, of the Grand Ballet du Marquis de Cuevas, dancing with this touring company an extensive and eclectic repertory with exemplary grace. Her performance in Balanchine's *Night Shadow* had an especial poetry, in which as the sleepwalking heroine she drifted over the stage guided by the hand of a poet who has fallen in love with her. In this beautiful ballet, Vyroubova's exquisite simplicity, and the emotion she could convey through her dreamlike dancing, was uniquely touching. It was Vyroubova's exceptional range and the unforced grandeur of her dancing which so excited audiences. In roles as varied as Lifar's Phèdre, as Giselle and the Sylphide, in Lifar's *Fourberies,* in which she was deliciously naughty, or in the stunning bravura of the *pas de trois* from *Paquita* (in which she and Hightower were matched by the virtuoso Serge Golovine), Vyroubova showed why she was revered as one of the great ballerinas of the century. She retired in 1965.

The Grand Ballet du Marquis de Cuevas was the last of the exotic and cosmopolitan ballet companies to exist without any state subvention (the de Cuevas company was supported by the Rockefeller fortune of the Marquis's wife). Essentially French-based, it welcomed many international stars and throughout the near two decades of its existence projected an image of international *chic* and glamour, winning a devoted audience throughout Europe and North Africa. One ballerina was central to the company's success as its enduring and dazzling star. This was Rosella Hightower, who was born in Oklahoma in 1920 and made her début with the Ballet Russe de Monte Carlo in 1938. She subsequently moved to American Ballet Theatre, and her years with these two companies were a good preparation for her emergence as the ballerina of the de Cuevas troupe in 1947.

Like Vyroubova, Hightower did much to restore the international reputation and identity of the French ballet. For the next fifteen years she created leading roles in

Right *Yvette Chauviré in Serge Lifar's* Nauteos *as staged at the Paris Opéra in 1954.*
Below *Nina Vyroubova in Serge Lifar's* Dramma per Musica, *first staged for the Nouveau Ballet de Monte Carlo in 1946 and subsequently revived at the Paris Opéra in 1950 when Vyroubova assumed the leading role. The décor was by Cassandre.*
Previous page *Vyroubova in* La Mort de Narcisse *with the Grand Ballet du Marquis de Cuevas.*

many ballets, and also danced the classic repertory. There was, in everything she performed, an astounding virtuosity placed at the service of the choreography. That her dancing had exceptional power by reason of its sheer technical excellence is testified by the stunning effects she achieved in the Black Swan *pas de deux*, where her *pirouettes à la grande seconde* (turns in which one leg was extended horizontally) have never been rivalled in clarity or exhilarating panache. That her assurance as a dancer was never gratuitous was seen in the mysterious *Piège de Lumière* (*Light Trap*), a ballet by John Taras with whom she often collaborated in the de Cuevas company. Set in the South American jungle, it showed convicts catching giant moths and butterflies by means of light traps: as a brilliantly exotic butterfly, Hightower flashed over the stage with extraordinary emotional effect. The sign of Hightower's dancing

Right *Rosella Hightower as the queen of the morphidae in* Piège de Lumière. *This ballet, first produced in 1952 for the Grand Ballet du Marquis de Cuevas, was one of the company's most important creations, and the high point of Hightower's collaborative partnership with John Taras as choreographer.* Far right *Rosella Hightower teaching at her school, the Centre International de Danse in Cannes.*

in every role was its grandeur of impulse, its largeness of scale and Hightower's own generosity of spirit as an interpreter and as a person.

On her retirement from dancing Rosella Hightower opened a school in Cannes which she has made one of the most important in Europe. She was for two years director of the ballet at the Paris Opéra before being succeeded by Rudolf Nureyev – with whom she had danced the Black Swan *pas de deux* in his first appearance in London at a charity gala.

Whatever the artistic uncertainties that the Paris Opéra knew after Lifar finally left the theatre in 1958 – and several directors have sought to control this extravagant if splendid company – one factor has remained constant. This is the unchanged excellence of the instruction in the Opéra School. The desire to excel, and the willingness

to work for technical polish, seems to be a national trait among French dancers; the French ballet scene has always been marked by the quality of its training and the quality of the dancers produced by that training. Today it must be said that the Paris Opéra knows a golden age of ballerinas and *premiers danseurs*. Under the direction of Rudolf Nureyev the company has greatly expanded its repertory and a profusion of talent has been put on display. Among the ballerinas, pride of place must be given to the senior *étoile* (the Paris troupe is rigorously categorised through the ranks of *stagiaires, quadrilles, coryphées, sujets, premiers danseurs* and the literal and actual stars, the *étoiles*), Noëlla Pontois.

Educated at the Opéra Ballet School, Pontois joined the company at the age of seventeen in 1960. A dancer of delicate physique and exceptional purity, she was made an *étoile* in 1968. The clarity of her style and its refined precision, combined with an effortless virtuosity, give delightful freshness and lightness to her interpretations. Her classic repertory – Giselle, Aurora, Odette-Odile, Raymonda – is performed with a beautiful ease and a gently feminine delicacy. Nothing seems impossible and, indeed, her dancing makes such light of difficulties that what touches the observer most is the elegant charm with which she speaks the language of the classic dance. She is a dancer of rare quality, a perfect representative of her national style.

Among Pontois's many gifted colleagues is Elisabeth Platel, who was a product of the Conservatoire Supérieure in Paris and then of the Opéra School. She entered the Opéra Ballet in 1976 at the age of seventeen and within five years she had been promoted to *étoile*. She is a ballerina of ideal physique; with her exquisite legs and feet and her perfectly placed head she is supremely fitted for the classic repertory. In everything her dancing is marked by a lightness and an exceptional concentration of

Opposite left *Noëlla Pontois as the heroine in Rudolf Nureyev's staging of* Raymonda.
Opposite right *Elisabeth Platel and Jean-Pierre Franchetti in Pierre Lacotte's staging of* La Sylphide.
This page left *Sylvie Guillem with Eric Vu-An in the* Mouvement, Rhythme, Etude *which Maurice Béjart made for them in 1985.*
This page right *Sylvie Guillem, youngest* étoile *of the Paris Opéra in 1986, in the* Grand Pas Classique *which Victor Gsovsky created in 1949 for Yvette Chauviré.*

emotion. Her Aurora is one of the very finest of our time, and in others of the nineteenth-century classics – *Swan Lake, Raymonda, Giselle* and *La Bayadère* – she demonstrates that inevitable rightness and distinction which mark the true ballerina. She has also been seen to extraordinary effect in Pierre Lacotte's reconstruction of the Taglioni ballet, *La Sylphide*, in which her airy grace and gentle charm brought Taglioni to life again. She performs much of the contemporary repertory, but both temperament and technique mark her as one of those rare beings who are destined to keep alive the flame of the classic repertory.

The youngest of the Opéra's *étoiles* is Sylvie Guillem. In December 1984, only five days after being promoted to the rank of *première danseuse*, Sylvie Guillem danced *Swan Lake* at the age of nineteen. In the hallowed tradition of the Paris Opéra, she was nominated as *étoile* after that performance, thereby becoming one of the youngest dancers ever to win this status.

The young Sylvie Guillem had taken up dancing after childhood experience in gymnastics. It was the director of the Paris Opéra School, Claude Bessy, a former *étoile*, who noticed the girl's exceptional gifts, and by the time she was fifteen she had been marked out even in the Opéra's school performances by the security of her technique and her precocious mastery of dance. She is possessed of an exceptionally free physique; her extensions are prodigious as her legs flash out in breath-taking lines. Maurice Béjart's pairing of her with the young *danseur* Eric Vu-An, in *Mouvement, Rhythme, Etude*, has drawn one of the most intriguing portraits of this young *étoile*. She offers her choreographer a slender and infinitely flexible body, and her suppleness and control are explored in solos and duets intensified by the extraordinary concentration which she brings to dancing.

The Royal Ballet

The history of Britain's Royal Ballet provides many insights into the importance attached to the ballerina tradition and, indeed, into the way ballerinas are created. It is significant that when, in 1926, Ninette de Valois approached Lilian Baylis, director of the Old Vic Theatre, with the improbable idea of establishing an English Ballet there, she had already taken the important first step of starting a ballet school. De Valois' Academy of Choreographic Art may have seemed inconsiderable when compared with the great academies in Russia, Copenhagen or Paris, but nevertheless it placed at the centre of the company of which she was then only dreaming a school which would produce the dancers she needed. Further, by approaching Lilian Baylis, de Valois recognised the need to place her putative troupe within the security of a repertory company that was not dependent upon the vagaries of commercial management; the existing achievements of the Old Vic Theatre as a home for the performance of drama and opera in tandem were proof enough of the soundness and good sense of an organisation which was in effect, if not in subsidy, already a national theatre. When in 1931 Miss Baylis acquired the rebuilt Sadler's Wells Theatre as a second home for her companies, it became the base for Ninette de Valois' school, and for her troupe of six professional dancers who were to become the embryo of the national ballet company that is now the Royal Ballet.

Ninette de Valois' decision to invite Alicia Markova to join her company, then known as the Vic-Wells Ballet, as her ballerina was also a significant one. This young English girl, who was still only twenty, had been formed in the Russian School and was heir to its traditions: without her presence de Valois would not have been able to bring her young company so firmly into the mainstream of the classic ballet. Thus it was that *Swan Lake* Act II was staged as an early classic test piece, and within three years *Giselle, The Nutcracker* and the full-length *Swan Lake* were added to the Vic-Wells Ballet's repertory for Markova.

The stagings, prepared by Nicholas Sergeyev from his own priceless Imperial Ballet notations, were accurate and entirely respectful reproductions in the style of the originals as he had supervised them while stage manager (*régisseur*) at the Mariinsky Theatre in St Petersburg. Today, when so many versions of the old ballets have been deformed by producers, and traduced by male dancers to provide themselves with increased dance opportunities, it is important to remember that the nineteenth-century ballet repertory was dominated by the ballerina, who was its sole justification. De Valois, who possessed a true classic ballerina in Markova, knew that she could show these works properly, and would have in them a rich storehouse for the future; they would serve to educate her dancers and her audience, and the example of Markova would provide the necessary model of technical and dramatic performance to which future ballerinas, when they were produced from within her company, could refer. And so it has proved.

Markova's Giselle, Odette-Odile, and Sugar Plum Fairy were the guarantee for the early success of the Vic-Wells Ballet as a classic enterprise. Her artistry was also admirably displayed in a large modern repertory that ranged from the enchanting lightness of *Les Rendezvous*, which Frederick Ashton created for her in 1933, to the pathos of her Betrayed Girl in de Valois' *The Rake's Progress* in 1935.

When, in 1935, Markova left the Vic-Wells organisation to form the Markova-Dolin Ballet (and to tour tirelessly for two years, thereby forming a new public for British ballet outside London), de Valois was able to share her roles among several young dancers who were graduating from her school. Chief among these was a part-Brazilian, part-English girl who had arrived at the school from Shanghai with the unballetic name of Peggy Hookham. That she was talented was evident. With a change of name, and ready to take up the opportunities left by Markova's departure, within the repertory enriched by Markova's performances, the seventeen-year-old Margot Fonteyn began her illustrious career.

By a fortunate conjunction of events, in this same year Ninette de Valois decided to add a resident choreographer to the roster of her company. She no longer had time to meet the company's needs for new ballets herself, and in Frederick Ashton, who had already created roles for Markova, she found an artist who possessed the classical taste and temperament to provide it with the repertory works it required. Ashton, born in 1904, had made his first choreography while a student at Marie Rambert's school. His was the first major talent that this exceptional woman discovered (others were Antony Tudor, Andrée Howard and Walter Gore) and, after working briefly in Paris, Ashton became a vital influence on the first efforts of the infant British ballet as the 1930s dawned. His choreographic collaboration with Margot Fonteyn, which lasted for more than a quarter of a century, produced a superlative collection of ballerina roles, and forms one of the brightest pages in the history of Britain's national ballet.

Fonteyn's progress towards her rank as prima ballerina of the Royal Ballet came through the double demands posed by the great ballerina roles and the creations made for her by Ashton. In everything her exceptional gifts were apparent: a physical frame that was beautifully balanced, its proportions ideal for classical dancing and so shaped that it avoided unnecessary physical stress; an impeccable musical sense which meant that the dance and the score were united in her interpretations; and a dramatic flair which meant that in the roles created for her by Ashton – Cinderella, Sylvia, Ondine, Chloë and many more – there was a sense of emotional rightness and poetic nuance that has never been touched by any other interpreter.

As the years progressed, Fonteyn was able to pare away more and more from her roles to reveal more and more of their essence, both technical and dramatic. So it was with her two greatest classic interpretations, Aurora in *The Sleeping Beauty* and Odette-Odile in *Swan Lake*: in both she epitomised the best qualities of the English style of dancing. There was no excessive bravura (Fonteyn was never a virtuoso), but the life of the dance and the life of the role were thrillingly present on stage: her Aurora blossomed from shy young princess to radiant bride; her Odette grieved and her Odile enchanted, and we understood the truth of the character and of the dance.

In the repertory of roles created for her by Ashton, we can see a symbiotic relationship at work between choreographer and artist: in shaping her talent, he was also inspired by it. In *Symphonic Variations* in 1946, Ashton makes a very deliberate statement about the self-sufficiency and beauty of the academic dance. The work calls for three ballerinas (Fonteyn, May and Shearer in the first performance) to display the poetic sensitivity of the English style: it is the role created by Fonteyn that is the focus for the work, representing the ideal of what Ashton thought British classic dancing should be. *Cinderella* (1948) and *Sylvia* (1952) also offered wonderful portraits of his ballerina, but it is *Ondine* (1958) which makes the culminating statement about their unique partnership, exploiting the full range of Fonteyn's musicality and her ability to suggest both innocent joy and the most searching grief. These qualities are woven into the text of the choreography to give the most rounded and bewitching portrayal of a great artist in her prime by a great choreographer in his prime. We are fortunate to have in Paul Czinner's film of *Ondine* a truthful record of a ballerina in one of her finest roles, one of the rare occasions that cinema has successfully preserved a unique balletic performance for posterity.

Margot Fonteyn and Rudolf Nureyev in Swan Lake *with the Royal Ballet. Previous page Fonteyn as Ondine in the ballet that Frederick Ashton created as a superlative tribute to her art.*

As Sadler's Wells Ballet began to grow in stature, Fonteyn was not called upon to carry the load of the repertory alone. Ninette de Valois's school was producing young dancers of distinction, led by Pamela May, Moira Shearer and Beryl Grey. This generation of ballerinas – as varied in gifts as they were complementary – formed a pleiad of talent around Fonteyn. Their working lives, like Fonteyn's, were very hard during the war years, when the Sadler's Wells company performed incessantly, on occasion giving three performances a day, struggling with food rationing, the absence of male dancers who had been called up for military service, and the terrors of air raids. Nevertheless, the Sadler's Wells Ballet went on tour (it had to flee from Holland in 1940 when the German army invaded the Low Countries), and the company brought ballet to a new audience round Britain, who found in it an ideal escape from the grim conditions of wartime.

Pamela May was a noble classical dancer, outstanding as Aurora (a role which admirably showed off her beautiful line), but also an adorable Swanilda in *Coppélia* and a powerful Odette-Odile. When she had retired from dancing, she lent lustre to the mime roles of the Princess Mother in *Swan Lake* and the Queen in *The Sleeping Beauty*. Moira Shearer's red-haired beauty was to win her fame in the cinema, notably in *The Red Shoes,* a film which encouraged many people to go to the ballet, but in

the theatre it was her dazzling, light technique and her speed which made her so rewarding an interpreter of Aurora and of Cinderella (in Ashton's production); while as the ballerina in his *Scènes de Ballet* and in Balanchine's *Ballet Imperial* she was also memorably good. Beryl Grey joined the company from its school in 1941 at the age of fourteen, and on her fifteenth birthday danced the full-length *Swan Lake*. This phenomenal achievement – her interpretation was technically excellent and emotionally touching – was the starting point of a distinguished career. *Giselle* followed in 1944 and she danced her first Lilac Fairy and Aurora in *The Sleeping Beauty* in 1946 when the Sadler's Wells Ballet moved to Covent Garden. A dancer of commanding height, Beryl Grey used her expansive and beautiful line to notable effect in the classical roles, and in such created roles as Death in Massine's *Donald of the Burthens* and, especially, as the Winter Fairy in *Cinderella*.

A welcome addition to this galaxy of ballerinas at the end of the war was Violetta Elvin. Born and trained in Moscow, she had danced as Violetta Prokhorova with the Bolshoi Ballet but, following her marriage to the English writer Harold Elvin, she settled in London and joined the Sadler's Wells Ballet, making her début as Princess Florine in the Blue Bird *pas de deux* on the second night of the 1946 Covent Garden season. Thereafter she was to illuminate many ballerina roles – notably in *Swan Lake*,

Far left *Pamela May as the Rich Girl in Frederick Ashton's* Nocturne. *Her costume, by Sophie Fedorovitch, is an admirable foil to her beauty.*
Centre *Moira Shearer backstage before a performance of* Les Sylphides *at the Royal Opera House, Covent Garden.*
Left *Beryl Grey and John Field in the third act of* Swan Lake.

Giselle and *The Sleeping Beauty*, in which the breadth and dignity of the Soviet style were greatly admired. Her created repertory of roles included La Morte Amoureuse in Ashton's *Don Juan* and Lykanion in his *Daphnis and Chloë* and made fine use of her great physical beauty and the intensity of feeling with which she coloured every characterisation.

In 1946 the company, still known as the Sadler's Wells Ballet, moved to a permanent home at the Royal Opera House, Covent Garden. The theatre's stage, much larger than any they had previously known, placed new demands on the dancers which they successfully answered. The artistry of Fonteyn, May, Shearer, Grey and Elvin was never more valuable than in the post-war years when the Sadler's Wells Ballet attained national status and national importance, and, in 1949, conquered New York on a crucial tour which allowed America to see the excellence of the 'dancing British'.

It was the particular achievement of these dancers that they handed on to the next generation of Sadler's Wells ballerinas an understanding of the repertory of classic ballets, as well as the new full-length works which Ashton was making, in what was in effect a line of succession from Petipa; *Cinderella, Sylvia, Ondine, La Fille mal gardée* and *The Two Pigeons*. The company's rising young artists were led by Nadia Nerina and Svetlana Beriosova, with their colleagues Elaine Fifield, Anya Linden, Rowena Jackson, Annette Page and Maryon Lane, many of whom first learned their craft in the 'second company', the Sadler's Wells Theatre Ballet which Ninette de Valois wisely initiated to serve as a nursery and proving ground.

Nerina was born in South Africa and came to Britain as soon as the war ended, eager to work and make a career with a national ballet company. She was invited to join the Sadler's Wells Theatre Ballet in 1946 but within a year had been recruited to the Covent Garden company where she became recognised as a virtuoso of buoyant style and radiant physical prowess. She danced all the leading roles in the classic repertory, and in Ashton's full-length works, to great acclaim. Always looking for a way to take dance to a larger audience, she appeared frequently on television and made important concert tours with her partner, Alexis Rassine. The most enchanting and happily enduring portrait we have of her is as Lise in *La Fille mal gardée,* a ballet which Ashton created for her and her partner David Blair in 1960. In Lise's soaring entries, in the bravura demands of the partnering, in the joyous sincerity of the characterisation and in the sunlit happiness of the ballet we see Nerina's qualities as they delighted audiences throughout the West and in Russia, where she was invited to dance with the Bolshoi and the Kirov Ballets, as Grey had done before her.

Svetlana Beriosova was born into a dancing family (her father is the ballet master Nicholas Beriozoff). She joined the Sadler's Wells Theatre Ballet in 1950 and two years later, at the age of twenty-one, transferred to the Covent Garden company. There she was revealed as a classical ballerina, eloquent and noble in *Swan Lake* and *The Sleeping Beauty*, but also most beguiling as Swanilda in *Coppélia*. Her dignity and the grace of her manner in the major classics were matched by the warmth she brought to the heroine of John Cranko's first full-length ballet, *The Prince of the*

Top *Violetta Elvin in the second act of* Swan Lake. *She was the first Bolshoi-trained dancer to be seen in London.*

Above *Svetlana Beriosova as Aurora, a portrait study which says everything about the beauty of this ballerina.*

Right *Nadia Nerina with Erik Bruhn in the* pas de deux *from* Don Quixote *during Bruhn's guest season with the Royal Ballet at Covent Garden in 1962.*

Pagodas, staged by the Royal Ballet in 1957, and her emotional intensity in two very differing roles – as Ashton's Persephone and Cranko's Antigone. Her mature abilities as an actress dancer were excellently seen in the creations of Lady Elgar in Ashton's *Enigma Variations* and as the Tsarina in Kenneth MacMillan's full-length *Anastasia.*

What must be seen as the Royal Ballet's third generation of ballerinas came in the form of a quartet of very talented girls who graduated from the Royal Ballet School in the mid-1950s; Merle Park, Lynn Seymour, Antoinette Sibley and Doreen Wells. Their careers and their gifts were remarkably contrasted. Merle Park, with a very bright, musical technique, was the first dancer to accept the challenge of Nerina's created role of Lise. She was also seen as a sparkling Aurora, and as Giselle and Odette-Odile, and was later to create the role of Clara in Rudolf Nureyev's staging of *The Nutcracker* for the Royal Ballet, but the full range of her vivid dramatic style was best appreciated in two major roles made for her by Kenneth MacMillan: as the Countess Larisch in *Mayerling* (1978) and as Isadora Duncan in *Isadora* (1981).

The course of Canadian-born Lynn Seymour's career was set when, in 1958, Kenneth MacMillan chose her for a leading role in his early work *The Burrow.* Her exquisite line and the intensity of her expressive gifts thereafter made her MacMillan's muse. His roles for her, from *Le Baiser de la Fée* in 1960 and *The Invitation* in 1961, to Mary Vetsera in *Mayerling* in 1978, showed a dramatic artist of great power and extreme sensitivity. No British ballerina, apart from Fonteyn, has had so many roles created for her. The fluidity of her style and her temperamental power were allied to an exceptionally musical sensitivity, best seen in her portrayals of MacMillan's Juliet and Anastasia as well as the girl in Ashton's *The Two Pigeons,* his Natalya in *A Month in the Country,* and in his *Brahms Waltzes in the Manner of Isadora Duncan.*

Right *Merle Park in her created role as Isadora Duncan in Kenneth MacMillan's* Isadora, *staged by the Royal Ballet at Covent Garden in 1981.*
Far right *Lynn Seymour as the young girl in the first act of Ashton's* The Two Pigeons, *a role she created in 1961.*
Inset *Lynn Seymour as Anna Anderson and Georgina Parkinson as the Tsarina in the third act of Kenneth MacMillan's* Anastasia: *in her fantasy world, Anna Anderson is seeking to establish her identity as the Grand Duchess Anastasia.*

Left *Galina Samsova as Aurora with London Festival Ballet in 1968.*
Below *Antoinette Sibley as Manon in the title role of Kenneth
Macmillan's ballet* Manon *which she created with the Royal Ballet at
Covent Garden in 1974.*
Bottom *Doreen Wells and David Wall as the young lovers in Ashton's*
The Two Pigeons, *a charming pose which fully displays the éclat their
partnership brought to the Touring Section of the Royal Ballet.*

Antoinette Sibley, Seymour's contemporary, first came to notice when she appeared as Swanilda in the first matinée given at Covent Garden by the Royal Ballet School in 1959. Her Odette-Odile which followed in 1960 gave confirmation that here was a dancer of rare classic distinction and her interpretations of all the great ballerina roles over the years have been illuminated by the purity of her style and her elegance. Her partnership with Anthony Dowell was of central importance to the Royal Ballet; in ballets ranging from MacMillan's *Manon*, which was created for the duo in 1974, to Ashton's *The Dream*, which initiated their partnership in 1964, Sibley and Dowell have epitomised the English style, and in many other works, classic and modern, Sibley's dancing has been the ideal realisation of those qualities of musicality, classic decorum and dramatic sensitivity which are the stylistic hallmark of the Royal Ballet.

The careers of Park, Seymour and Sibley were all, to a great extent, firmly centred on the Royal Ballet in its home at the Royal Opera House. The career of Doreen Wells, their contemporary, tells of the importance of the touring section of Britain's national ballet and the vital influence of a leading ballerina in winning a lasting and devoted public following for the company. Doreen Wells joined the Sadler's Wells Theatre Ballet in 1955. She danced for a brief period with the Covent Garden section of the Royal Ballet and then, in 1960, became ballerina with the Royal Ballet touring section, where she was to remain for the next fourteen years.

A dancer of enchanting prettiness and lightness, blonde and blue-eyed, as greatly admired in the classics as in the modern repertory, Doreen Wells introduced many to the vivid delights of ballet-going and came to represent for a huge audience around Britain and Europe the excellence of standards set by the Royal Ballet. As Lise in *La Fille mal gardée* or as Aurora in *The Sleeping Beauty* and the Young Girl in *The Two Pigeons*, she gave performances of abiding charm: the ardours of a touring life and the exhaustion of constant travel did nothing to diminish the sweetness and grace of her interpretations. David Wall was her partner, and for many years the couple were, in every role, ideal ambassadors for their art.

The present-day leaders of the Royal Ballet companies include Lesley Collier, whose sure technique in the classical roles is matched by the conviction of her performances in the dramatic works of Kenneth MacMillan; Jennifer Penney, who possesses an ideally proportioned body for a ballerina; and a younger generation, led by Fiona Chadwick, Bryony Brind, Maria Almeida and Ravenna Tucker. With the Sadler's Wells Royal Ballet, the Russian-born Galina Samsova (who joined the company in 1979, having already won international acclaim with various other companies) has proved a shining example of the true ballerina manner in classical roles, while the very different and younger dancers, versatile Marion Tait and romantic Margaret Barbieri, now share ballerina roles with New Zealand-born Sherilyn Kennedy and the even younger aspirants Sandra Madgwick, Karen Donovan and Leanne Benjamin.

Balanchine and American Ballet

The first authentically American ballerinas were stars of the Romantic Age. Augusta Maywood (1825–76), who was born in New York, made her career in Europe, dancing at the Paris Opéra and touring widely – she staged a version of *Uncle Tom's Cabin* for her Italian audiences. Mary Ann Lee (1823–99) studied in Paris but made her career in her native land. She is best known for having been the first American Giselle, dancing the role only four years after Grisi had created it in Paris. However, by far the greater number of ballerinas in America for the next century were European stars, like Elssler and Pavlova. Indeed, during the extended American tours of the Ballets Russes companies in the 1930s audiences became so accustomed to such names as Danilova, Markova, Toumanova, Baronova and Riabouchinska that ballet for the great American public meant 'Russian ballet', and it was the task of George Balanchine with his patron and associate Lincoln Kirstein to show eventually that it could be, and was, an American art.

It was at Lincoln Kirstein's invitation in 1933 that George Balanchine left Europe to come to America to found a school and form a company. The history of their work together is the history of that great academy, the School of American Ballet, and of the New York City Ballet which had emerged, by 1948, as the performing ensemble we know today. The other major American troupe, American Ballet Theatre, was created in 1939 (as Ballet Theatre) and gave its first performance in January 1940: its ideals and history are in direct contrast to those of the New York City Ballet.

Born in St Petersburg in 1904, George Balanchine studied ballet at the Imperial School in his native city. He graduated into the post-Revolutionary State Ballet there, but in 1924 left Russia and was recruited by Diaghilev in the same year as final ballet master for the Ballet Russe. In a celebrated comment, Balanchine declared that 'ballet is woman' and by far the greater proportion of his ballets were concerned to show women dancing. But Balanchine also believed that the choreography was far more important than any artist, and in the New York City Ballet the primacy of the choreographer was never in doubt. He did not wish for any of that 'star' behaviour which he had known with the Ballet Russe companies, nor for the spectacles of ballets created as 'star' vehicles to show off the qualities, temperaments and personal allure of the great ballerina. He aimed consciously to create a ballet company which studiously avoided any sort of stellar ranking of performers or the sacrifice of its identity to the identity of a 'star': the company itself and its choreography were the stars. Furthermore, he wished to eschew all the emotional and nostalgic elements associated with the idea of 'the ballerina' – the Dying Swan, the Swan Queen, the bewitched Princess, the consoling Ghost. For him, as he arrived in America in 1933 to set about making classic ballet an American art, America's young girls 'were not Sylphides; they were basket-ball champions and queens of the tennis court, whose proper domain was athletics. They were long-legged, long-necked, slim-hipped, and capable of endless acrobatic virtuosity. The drum majorette, the cheer-leader of the High School football team of the 1930s filled his eye ...' Thus Lincoln Kirstein described the ideals that informed the dance style and the ideas of the dancers which Balanchine used to make his great company.

There emerged a repertory and a style absolutely coherent as a view of what dance and dancing should be. Balanchine sought to extend the capabilities of the classic academic style which he brought from his Imperial Russian training and his European experience by making it 'American' in its speed, clarity and muscular drive, and intensely responsive to music (as he was himself as a choreographer). His ideal was a selfless dancer who devoted herself to the choreography and whose identity would be defined by the choreography: in discussing an ideal of a dancer he wrote, 'We will remember the girl but only because of the dance she showed us.'

But it would be unrealistic to suppose that Balanchine's dancers were no more than automata obedient to the mechanical invention of their master. He did not wish for the strong flavour of stellar temperament and stellar mannerisms, but his leading dancers were ballerinas, and stars as potent in their way as any created within the traditions of the Ballet Russe. Thus we can write of such Balanchine 'star dancers' and ballerinas as Maria Tallchief, Melissa Hayden, Tanaquil LeClercq, Patricia Wilde, Diana Adams, Violette Verdy, Allegra Kent, Patricia MacBride, Suzanne Farrell, Merrill Ashley, Karin von Aroldingen, Kay Mazzo, Gelsey Kirkland, Kyra Nichols, Maria Calegari, Darci Kistler and many more, and contemplate a list of performers as exciting and varied in gifts as in any other company in the world.

These artists, these ballerinas, were displayed in a repertory which in richness of creativity, daring and classic power is unrivalled in this century. Balanchine, master choreographer of our age, the heir to Petipa and the man who, by his genius, has given twentieth-century classic dancing its true and most brilliant image, produced a dazzling succession of ballets in which his leading female dancers – his ballerinas – were wonderfully shown, both as artists of exceptional variety of physical style and talent and as servants – or partners – of the choreographic imagination of Balanchine.

Any account of Balanchine's greatest ballets can serve as a survey of his leading ballerinas. Maria Tallchief in his staging of *The Firebird* (1949) was hailed by the critic John Martin: 'Undoubtedly, Tallchief has been his [Balanchine's] inspiration. Hers is the key role, and he has built for her astonishing virtuosity almost as if he were challenging it. Yet there is nothing of the circus in it; there are fabulous acrobatic tricks in it, but they are invariably justified by the fact that the role is that of a magic bird who has been captured and is struggling for her freedom. Tallchief keeps this

Maria Tallchief as the Firebird in Balanchine's first version of the Stravinsky score for New York City Ballet.
Previous page *George Balanchine rehearsing his Variations (set to Stravinsky's Variations in Memory of Aldous Huxley) with the young Suzanne Farrell. The ballet used Stravinsky's brief, 8-minute score and played it three times: it was in the third reprise that Balanchine made one of his early studies of Suzanne Farrell's dancing.*

always before us, and as she gives us each of the choreographer's inventions, he is ready with another for her, as if he were actually feeding creatively on her performance. Certainly we have never seen a *Firebird* performed and choreographed with such uncanny unity.'

John Martin's wise words indicate a truth greater than his record of Tallchief's glorious creation: Balanchine fed from his ballerina and in return fed her – using her abilities, but also setting them fresh and dazzling new challenges. This has ever been part of the collaboration of ballerina and choreographer, but in the Balanchine repertory – as in the work of Ashton and Fonteyn, MacMillan and Seymour, Cranko and Marcia Haydée – we witness it at its most intense and fascinating.

For Tanaquil LeClercq, Balanchine's portrait was at once a poetic and an extraordinary one. In her survey of the New York City Ballet repertory, *Repertory in Review*, Nancy Reynolds gives this view of LeClercq in Balanchine's version of *La Valse*. A girl in white enters a ballroom, and as Ravel's apotheosis of the Viennese Waltz whirls onward she is chosen by Death as a partner, donning the gauzy black cloak, black gloves and jewels that he gives her. '*La Valse* may have been the

Right *Tanaquil LeClercq and Nicholas Magallanes in* Jones Beach, *a ballet jointly choreographed by Balanchine and Robbins in 1949, which was a light-hearted view of young people enjoying themselves on a beach near New York.*
Far right *Allegra Kent in Balanchine's staging of* Swan Lake *for New York City Ballet. Balanchine's one-act* Swan Lake *is very different from any other version – a comment upon the original Ivanov lakeside scene, which receives from such New York City Ballet principals as Allegra Kent readings of the greatest beauty and classic distinction.*

quintessential role of LeClercq, not only for its angular sophistication and doomed half innocence, which she was superbly equipped to project, but for the eerie parallel between her waltz with Death and her real-life paralysis from polio in 1956.' The ballet was created in 1951 and immediately gripped audiences by its vivid theatrical sense – Balanchine was a master of balletic drama when he chose. Five years later Tanaquil LeClercq was paralysed by poliomyelitis, the cruellest fate imaginable for a ballerina. Sustained by Balanchine, who was then her husband, LeClercq gradually returned to the ballet world, teaching and coaching from her wheelchair.

The roles he made for the French-born ballerina Violette Verdy, in the Emeralds section of *Jewels* (1967) and in the *Tchaikovsky Pas de Deux* (1960), are drawn with an evident affection and admiration for her enchanting femininity, her brilliant technique and her prodigious musical sensitivity. She 'became' the music, inhabiting it, breathing it, as have few other dancers in our experience. For Melissa Hayden, a series of ballets explored her powerful skills, culminating in the *Cortège Hongrois* of 1973, which marked her farewell to the stage and which Balanchine conceived as a tribute to a ballerina of full and grandiose style.

For another exceptional artist, Allegra Kent, Balanchine's repertory provided two contrasting portraits: that of a pliant *danseuse* in the beautiful and mysterious *Episodes* (1959), set to music by Webern, in which Kent's yielding plasticity was wonderfully used: and as the tragic sleepwalking heroine of *Night Shadow* (1946) in which, as the somnambulist who attracts a poet and unwittingly causes his death, she was the soul of mystery and of exquisite, elusive beauty, just as, in works as diverse as *Monumentum pro Gesualdo* (1960) and *Liebeslieder Walzer* (1960), Balanchine made magnificent use of the gifts of Diana Adams, a dancer of aristocratic and distinguished style, supremely seen in the *pas de deux* from *Agon* (1957). Among the leading ballerinas of the company today, Patricia MacBride's dazzling variety of style is displayed in roles as radically different from each other as the ballerina of the Rubies scherzo in *Jewels* (set to Stravinsky's *Capriccio for Piano and Orchestra*) in which she darts and dashes, entirely mistress of Balanchine's most advanced and even jazzy classic writing, and the Swanilda of his *Coppélia* (1974) or Columbine in his *Harlequinade* (1965), both of which she plays with delightful vivacity and humour.

But of all Balanchine's dancers during the past twenty-five years, it is Suzanne Farrell who was most essentially a muse for the great choreographer. In a marvellous catalogue of ballets, from his first major creation for her as Dulcinea in *Don Quixote* in 1965, when she was twenty, and in the Diamonds section in *Jewels* (Balanchine referred to the young Farrell as 'an alabaster princess'), to such late masterpieces as *Vienna Waltzes* (1977), *Robert Schumann's Davidsbündlertänze* (1980) and *Mozartiana* (1981), Balanchine extended and explored the range of Farrell's magnificent gifts as a classical dancer having few peers in the world today, and as an interpretative artist capable of the greatest musical and temperamental subtlety. One has but to contrast her serene grandeur in Diamonds with the dazzling virtuosity of her performance in Ravel's *Tzigane* (1975) or her potent sense of feeling and classic dignity in *Mozartiana* to see in their collaboration one of the great glories of ballet in the twentieth century.

That Balanchine could reveal unexpected and splendid facets of a dancer's art was also to be seen in his creations for the German-trained Karin von Aroldingen, who joined his company in 1962 and was for more than twenty years a leading artist of the troupe, notable for the powerful physical contribution she made to the repertory. Balanchine revealed both her ravishing sense of music in *Vienna Waltzes* in 1977 (von Aroldingen seeming to embody with effortless joy the pulse of the waltz tempo) and the aggressive power of her presence in *Stravinsky Violin Concerto* (1972), and also her compassionate, emotional beauty as the Clara Schumann figure in *Davidsbündlertänze,* a role which von Aroldingen played with a hushed and penetrating sensitivity.

For sheer speed, and a radiant prowess, New York City Ballet has never shown a dancer more brilliantly fleet than Merrill Ashley, and in two created ballets – as well as in the general repertory – Balanchine set challenges to this exceptional artist which she met with a joyous ease. In *Ballo della Regina* (1978), using Verdi ballet music, Balanchine produced a role demanding speed that seemed to dazzle the eye, and

Below *Suzanne Farrell as Terpsichore and Ib Andersen as the young god in Balanchine's* Apollo *as staged by New York City Ballet. (Compare the costume of today with the original production, p. 77)* Right *Patricia MacBride and Mikhail Baryshnikov in Jerome Robbins'* Other Dances. *Robbins originally made this duet for Natalia Makarova and Baryshnikov.*

clarity of articulation – the equivalent of fast, exquisitely precise pianism – which challenged Ashley and led her to display a dance of unprecedented and unmatched coloratura brilliance and exhilaration.

In 1980, with Ashley now celebrated for these qualities, Balanchine created a second ballet – *Ballade*, set to music by Fauré – in which a softer temperamental style and a womanly grace very different from the youthful bravura of *Ballo della Regina* showed how Ashley's clarity was undiminished but set her at the service of more gentle and passionate emotion.

Among the other leading artists currently at the New York City Ballet, Kyra Nichols stands out by dint of the sunny and perfectly rounded technique which she brings to every role and the radiant assurance which informs her dancing: in ballets such as *Suite No. 3* (1970), in which she dances the Theme and Variations, in *Piano Concerto No. 2* (1944), or in ballets created for her by Jerome Robbins – *The Four Seasons, Piano Pieces* – the beautiful serenity of her dancing, its warmth and generosity of style and its spiritual decorum (she is truly a selfless servant of movement, although her own delightful temperament is ever there to enchant the audience) make her an ideal representative of New York City Ballet manner. So, too, is the case with the work of Maria Calegari, a dancer who has blossomed both in the Balanchine and Robbins repertory: with her beautiful line and the purity, and sometimes elegant reserve, of her manner, she seems to move from a centre of clear understanding of the dance, setting out choreography with a precision that is uniquely part of the New

Left *Kyra Nichols and Joseph Duell in
Balanchine's* Liebeslieder Walzer. *Balanchine
choreographed the two sets of Brahms vocal
quartets as a ballet in 1960, producing one of
the loveliest and most ingenious of his works
concerned with waltz rhythm. Shown here is the
handsome revival of 1982 when the ballet was
given new designs.*

Above *Merrill Ashley in Balanchine's*
Donizetti Variations. *This photograph
captures something of the exhilarating speed
associated with Merrill Ashley's dancing. The
musical variations to which she dances are taken
from Donizetti's* Don Sebastian.

Above right *Maria Calegari in Balanchine's
loving realisation of George Gershwin tunes,*
Who Cares? *This was first given in 1970 and
has been an abiding delight in the repertory of
New York City Ballet ever since.*

Right *Darci Kistler and Sean Lavery in Peter
Martin's* Symphony No. 1 *for New York City
Ballet, set to Tchaikovsky's First Symphony.*

York City Ballet style. Darci Kistler, youngest of the company principals at the moment, is another dancer whose movement seems to have a reserve of brightest energy and technical assurance which exhilarates an audience. After a period of illness, she has returned to dancing, and as Titania in *A Midsummer Night's Dream* (1962) or in the traditional New York City Ballet repertory, she shows an amplitude and richness of manner which are enormously promising for the future.

One other New York City Ballet ballerina has to be mentioned here: Gelsey Kirkland, possessed of an exquisite physique, was one of the brightest hopes of the company, creating a sensation in her performance in Balanchine's setting of Tchaikovsky's *Suite No. 3* (1970), as the Firebird in his 1972 revision of the Stravinsky ballet, and as a soloist in Robbins's *Goldberg Variations*. These roles, and her repertory assignments, told of a young dancer (born in 1953, she was still in her teens) of prodigious gifts. In 1974 Kirkland left New York City Ballet to join American Ballet Theatre where she appeared in that company's more eclectic repertory, making a notable success in partnership with Baryshnikov in *Giselle,* and also appearing as a guest artist with the Royal Ballet as Juliet. Ill health curtailed her career, but a recent return to dancing has delighted audiences who rejoice in the dazzling technique and slightly fey quality of Kirkland's interpretations.

The New York City Ballet repertory continues to present – as it has always done – an exceptional variety of ballerinas and a wide range of women's roles: such works as Jerome Robbins's *Dances at a Gathering*, Balanchine's *Divertimento No. 15* and his subtle *Duo Concertant* tell of the glorious challenges and rewards to the ballerina (or the female principal and the female principle in ballet) in American classic dance. In contradistinction to New York City Ballet and its tradition of creating its own principals, American Ballet Theatre has relied very much upon the idea of imported dancers: Markova and Dolin, Baronova and Massine were early stars, and in later years Carla Fracci and Erik Bruhn, Natalia Makarova, Fernando Bujones and Mikhail Baryshnikov have been its greatest box-office draws. Of ballerinas who were initially associated with its triumphs one was completely home-grown: Nora Kaye. Another, Alicia Alonso, was to move eventually from Ballet Theatre to create the National Ballet in her native Cuba of which she remains the *assoluta*.

It is ironic that Nora Kaye was in fact born Nora Koreff – her Russian name would, in earlier times, have been a distinct advantage in the world of the Ballet Russe when it was felt necessary for artists to be re-christened: the English girl Hilda Munnings became the eminent Diaghilev artist Lydia Sokolova. Nora Kaye was an original member of American Ballet Theatre, and her gifts were realised in astonishing fashion when, in 1942, she was chosen by Antony Tudor (the great English cho-reographer who had been invited to join Ballet Theatre at its inception) for the leading role in his new ballet, and his first creation in America, *Pillar of Fire* (1942). As the heroine, Hagar, a woman frustrated and driven into unhappiness, but finally discovering a compassionate and rewarding love, Kaye gave a performance which announced to a delighted public that here was a superlative dance actress.

Left *Gelsey Kirkland as the Wili Giselle in the second act of the ballet.*
Below left *Alicia Markova and Erik Bruhn in* Les Sylphides *with American Ballet Theatre.*
Below *Nora Kaye as Hagar in Tudor's* Pillar of Fire *with American Ballet Theatre. The expressive force of Kaye's dancing is evident in this pose.*

Below *Nicholas Magallanes and Nora Kaye in Jerome Robbin's* The Cage, *staged for New York City Ballet in 1951 with these dancers as its original cast. The ballet shocked audiences by its brilliant evocation of an insect society in which the female 'considered the male as prey'.* Right *Alicia Alonso and Jorge Esquivel in* La Diva, *a ballet about Maria Callas, staged for the Cuban Ballet by Alberto Mendez.*

Writing in Charles Payne's magnificent history of the company, *American Ballet Theatre,* Kaye observed: 'Tudor's approach to creation was entirely different from that of any other choreographer. He had his own special method of probing a character's emotions and displaying them in dance form. He had me indicate Hagar's frustrated emotional state in the opening scene of *Pillar of Fire* with the simple gesture of raising my hand to my cheek. This gesture, however, was arrived at only after hours of probing. Tudor would say, "You live in such-and-such a town, you eat such-and-such food, you dress so-and-so, you have this sort of family, you live in this sort of house." Only after he (with me) had determined just what sort of a person Hagar was, did he begin to think how Hagar would move.'

This search for characterisation indicates the artistry and the truth of Nora Kaye's communicative gifts. As Lizzie Borden in Agnes de Mille's *Fall River Legend* (a ballet not noted for its subtlety of effect), Nora Kaye brought a brooding and terrible intensity to the role of the murderess – and a sense of compassion for the character she played which transcended the rather obvious theatricalities of the piece. It was these roles which earned Kaye the accolade of 'the Duse of the Dance', but her repertory also included the traditional classics and the acquisitions which marked American Ballet Theatre's every season. For a period of three years, 1951–54, Kaye joined New York City Ballet, where she created the leading role in Robbins's *The Cage,* a brilliantly realised revision of the second act of *Giselle* – a novice inducted into a group of insects, it would seem in this staging, who must destroy the men who enter this female domain – and also appeared in Tudor's *Lilac Garden* as Caroline, and created the role of the *monstre sacré* actress who was the heroine of his *La Gloire.*

The ballet itself was not a success – there was too much action and too little dance, overwhelmed by three Beethoven overtures – but Kaye herself brought blazing credibility to the role of the star actress who was the ballet's *raison d'être*.

American Ballet Theatre's other leading ballerina during the 1940s and 1950s was Alicia Alonso. Her story is one of the most remarkable in modern ballet history, a matter of triumph over obstacles, and dedication to the cause of a national ballet troupe. Born in Cuba in 1917, she studied dancing in Cuba and New York, where she had her early appearances in Broadway musicals before joining American Ballet Theatre in 1941. A dancer of exceptional technique and strong dramatic presence, she was hailed both in the classics (Giselle was among her most celebrated roles) and in the modern repertory – notably in such works created for her and her partner Igor Youskevitch as Balanchine's *Theme and Variations* (1947) and in Tudor's *Undertow* (1945) and *Shadow of the Wind* (1948). She danced the first performance of *Fall River Legend* and subsequently shared the role of Lizzie Borden with Nora Kaye, to considerable success.

In 1948 Alonso formed her own company in Havana, with which she danced while maintaining her relationship with American Ballet Theatre, but with the accession of Fidel Castro in 1959 this company became the National Ballet of Cuba, a troupe of international stature with a fine roster of ballerinas. Alonso, however, remains its *assoluta* and its inspiring figurehead – not least because of her exceptional bravery in contending with a disease of the eye which rendered her nearly blind. Indomitably, Alonso continued working and dancing, and her art and her passion for dance and for her native land have won worldwide acclaim for her performances and for her company. At an age when many another ballerina has retired, Alonso continued, astoundingly, to dance – in roles specially created for her and in *Giselle* – and, no matter what accommodation of technique has been necessary, the style and the blazing commitment of this remarkable ballerina have commanded the admiration and enthusiastic response of the public wherever she has appeared.

Of subsequent leading artists – and American Ballet Theatre's guests have included many leading ballerinas from Europe – Cynthia Gregory has proved one of the most popular and enduring of native principals. A gala performance in her honour in June 1985 during the company's season at the Metropolitan Opera House, New York, celebrated her twenty years with American Ballet Theatre. Some idea of Cynthia Gregory's range was given in a programme which contained extracts from the classics chosen to display her brilliant technique – *Coppélia*, *La Bayadère*, *Swan Lake*, *The Sleeping Beauty*, *Giselle*, *La Sylphide* and *Raymonda* – as well as works in modern choreography created for her by Twyla Tharp, Alvin Ailey, Denis Nahat, Eliot Feld, Michael Smuin, from the more than seventy works she has danced with the company. In Cynthia Gregory's career we see the importance of the 'all-round ballerina' to a company having a large and eclectic repertory: by virtue of her adaptability and an acute sense of stylistic difference, the leading resident ballerina exemplifies the dedication which is vital in sustaining the artistic standards of an ensemble.

The European Scene

In his obituary of August Bournonville, the Danish writer Edvard Brandes made the intriguing point that it was thanks to him that Denmark was the first country in the world in which the description *danseuse* was not synonymous with that of courtesan. In all the ballets he created for the Royal Danish Ballet, Bournonville sought to show that his heroines were decent and honourable women, and only in *La Sylphide* did he succumb (unwillingly) to the more fevered and, to him, 'unwholesome' ideals of the French Romantic movement. Otherwise the heroines we see in his ballets that survive today, Eleonora in *Kermesse in Bruges,* Teresina in *Napoli* and Hilda in *A Folk Tale*, are gentle, gracious girls, whose moral decency and sweetness of temperament is a proper reward for the hero. Bournonville's choreographic style also stressed these qualities: decorous charm, sweetness of pose, brightness and buoyancy of step were the qualities required of the *danseuse*. It may be said that the roles have their milk-and-water moments, that they do not plumb any great depths of tragedy, but to give them life, to make them as beguiling as they should be and to dance with the proper sprightliness and fluency calls for great skill: they are still very prettily and graciously performed in Denmark today.

It must also be noted that Bournonville's ballets and his training system (happily preserved since the 1830s) stressed male technique, and whereas in the rest of Europe male dancing fell on hard times and stony ground, the Danes continued to produce (as they do today) male dancers of exceptional talent who have most usually been the dominant figures in the repertory and the company. Svend Kragh Jacobsen, most eminent of Danish critics, wrote: 'Denmark has supplied few women dancers to the world élite,' yet there have been Danish ballerinas, famous nationally and internationally, who have won the affection and unstinted admiration of a huge public. Bournonville's own ballerinas were artists of delightful charm, witness Augusta Nielsen (1822–1902), and Juliette Price (1831–1906) and her niece Ellen Price (1879–1968), who were members of a distinguished dynasty of Danish dancers (with English ancestry, as their name suggests). Valborg Borchsenius (1872–1949) was another illustrious artist, responsible for helping to preserve much of the old Bournonville repertory.

In modern times, Margot Lander (1910–61) has been acclaimed as an ideal interpreter of the Danish repertory, a notable Giselle and an adorably witty Swanilda. In 1941 she was the first solodancer (as the Danes call their ballerinas) to be accorded the title of prima ballerina. Her successor was Margrethe Schanne (1921–   ), a

romantic artist whose dance style and training goes back, as Kragh Jacobsen observed, 'in unbroken tradition to Bournonville's favourite dancer, Juliette Price'. Schanne was admired for the delicacy and lightness of her dancing and for that rare ability to 'stir the soul without sentimentality': her interpretations as Giselle and La Sylphide were justly famed and appreciated by connoisseurs of the Romantic dance for the purity and elegance of her technique and the distinction of her style. Her contemporaries were Mona Vangsaae (1920–83), one of the first of the Danish ballerinas to profit, albeit towards the end of her career, from the teaching of Vera Volkova (an early pupil of Vaganova, who taught first in London and then for many years in Copenhagen: she was recognised as one of the most inspiring and gifted teachers of the century), and who was chosen by Ashton to create the role of Juliet in his *Romeo and Juliet*; and Inge Sand (1928–74), unrivalled in her generation as Swanilda. Of the next generation of Danish ballerinas, a special place is held by Kirsten Simone, a pupil of Volkova, who was noted both for her personal beauty, and for the dramatic clarity of her performances. Her subtle statement of Bournonville characters continues today in the great mime roles of the repertory.

One Danish ballerina, Toni Lander (1931–85), was to achieve a wholly international career. In Denmark she became a solodancer in her early twenties but by 1954 she

Far left *Valborg Borchsenius and Hans Beck in the second act of* La Sylphide.
Left *Margrethe Schanne in the mad scene of* Giselle, *with Henning Kronstam as Albrecht, in the late 1950s.*
Below *Toni Lander in Bournonville's* Napoli *as staged for Festival Ballet by her husband Harald Lander. Toni Lander was one of the greatest Danish dancers of her time and enjoyed an international career before her untimely death in 1985.*
Previous page *Margot Lander in the second act of* Giselle.

had joined London Festival Ballet, for which company she remained a ballerina for five years, demonstrating a grandeur and a beautiful simplicity of dancing – her every role being clear, clean and communicative of feeling. She was later to work with American Ballet Theatre and to return to Copenhagen as a guest with her parent company: a most vivid memory of her dancing (for she retired early and died tragically young) is in *Etudes,* a ballet celebrating the technique of the dancers' daily class choreographed by her first husband, Harald Lander. In the leading part, Toni Lander offered a brilliance and an elegance of presence which have never been equalled in this enduringly popular ballet.

Of the present generation of Royal Danish principals, the senior ballerinas are Mette Honnigen and Anna Laerkeson, who have been admired in both the Bournonville and

Lis Jeppesen as Hilda and Arne Villumsen as Junker Ove in Bournonville's A Folk Tale, *as staged during the Bournonville centenary festival of 1979 in Copenhagen. Hilda is about to offer Ove a draught of holy water which will restore his sanity – one of the central incidents of this beautiful Romantic ballet.*

contemporary repertory of their company. Of the young ballerinas, Mette Ida Kirk and Lis Jeppesen were first to be hailed in the traditional Bournonville repertory during the Bournonville centenary celebrations in Copenhagen in 1979 – they had the task, as did their seniors, of finding their own way of presenting the charms and grace of the heroines of *Kermesse in Bruges* and *A Folk Tale* and *La Sylphide*. When a repertory is as constricted in its range as is, inevitably, the surviving list of Bournonville ballets, the problems for the young artist in creating a vivid impression are considerable, but in the performances of these young dancers it is rewarding to see how such roles are both treasured for their historical worth – and enhanced by the innate traditions of the ballet company – and illuminated by new insights and fresh artistry. It is in this way that the old ballets – in Denmark and the Soviet Union, as throughout

the rest of the ballet world – grow and continue to stimulate interpreters and audiences.

A ballerina is fortunate if she becomes the muse for a choreographer. Her uncertainties about roles and her development as an artist are then shared and sometimes entirely handed over to the creative control of a ballet master. The artistic and spiritual traffic involved may not be, and should not be, one-sided, for the dancer's abilities are a challenge as well as an inspiration for the choreographer's energies. There results from this collaborative existence a clearer image of the ballerina, a sharpened identity, which no other guidance or help can replace. Thus we infer it was for Tamara Karsavina with Mikhail Fokine. Thus we have seen, gloriously, it has been with Suzanne Farrell and Balanchine at the New York City Ballet; with Margot Fonteyn and Frederick Ashton; with Natalia Bessmertnova and Yuri Grigorovich at the Bolshoi; and Lynn Seymour and Kenneth MacMillan at the Royal Ballet. And thus it was with Marcia Haydée and John Cranko. It was Marcia Haydée's additional good fortune to come into Cranko's creative life at exactly the right moment, just as he was setting about his task of rebuilding and turning the young Stuttgart company, where he had recently been appointed director, into a major ballet ensemble.

Born in Brazil, a contemporary in the 1950s of Sibley, Seymour and Park at the Royal Ballet School, Haydée's first professional work was with the Grand Ballet du Marquis de Cuevas. As the de Cuevas troupe entered its final season, Haydée decided to find work elsewhere and, recalling the pleasure she had known in dancing for Cranko when he staged a short ballet for the de Cuevas company, she applied to him for a job in Stuttgart. To her amazement, she was offered not a soloist contract but the post of leading ballerina. What Cranko sensed in Haydée was talent unsure and unfocused. He was to discover a dedication to work, an expressive passion and reserves of emotional and physical power, which would give the Stuttgart Ballet a star capable of justifying a repertory that came to include a series of vastly popular full-evening ballets – *Onegin*, *Romeo and Juliet* and *The Taming of the Shrew* – which Cranko made for her, as well as the traditional nineteenth-century repertory.

Between Marcia Haydée and John Cranko there developed a relationship of great importance to the Stuttgart Ballet. Shaped, coaxed and inspired by his understanding and aspiration for her gifts, she was to grow into an outstandingly expressive ballerina, her qualities burnished by Cranko's own ballets and by the ballets he also acquired for her from Kenneth MacMillan, able to provide his ensemble with a focus for the identity of the troupe. In her thrilling dramatic performances – as the poetic Tatiana in *Onegin,*who matured from dreaming girl to passionate woman; as a lyrical Juliet; as the adorably bellicose Katherine in *The Taming of the Shrew* – Haydée became one of the best-loved and most admired artists in European ballet, the epitome of the ballerina as expressive divinity.

After Cranko's death, in an aeroplane bringing his company back from a second triumphant visit to New York, Haydée's identification with the Stuttgart Ballet was further confirmed when she eventually became, as she remains, its director as well as

Eva Evdokimova as Odette in
Swan Lake.

star ballerina. She has inspired ballets by John Neumeier (*La Dame aux camélias* and *A Streetcar Named Desire*) and by Maurice Béjart (*Divine* and *Wien, Wien nur du allein*) which admirably display the qualities that first told John Cranko that he was in the presence of a rare artist: she communicates the external shape of the choreography with exceptional subtlety but, even more importantly, she persuades her audience of its inner life and fascination. She believes, and her audience believes with her.

Eva Evdokimova is an artist who has divided her time between several companies – notably the Ballet of the Deutsche Opera in Berlin, the Munich Ballet and London Festival Ballet. After studies at the Royal Ballet School in London and the Royal Danish Ballet School, where she worked with Vera Volkova, she won a gold medal at the Varna Ballet Competition in 1970, and realised her first great success as Giselle which she first danced with London Festival Ballet in that same year. Her delicate physique is suited to the Romantic repertory, and in the second act the natural 'voice' of her dancing gave the character of the Wili a feathery lightness and a gazelle-like spring. She conveyed then, as she was to do with far greater assurance as the years progressed, the vaporous nature of the ghostly Giselle and her compassionate love for Albrecht. When Peter Schaufuss staged the Bournonville version of *La Sylphide* for London Festival Ballet in 1979, her airy jump and *ballon* (that ability to spring sweetly and easily from the stage) gave ravishing outlines to the role. Evdokimova could hold an arabesque so that she seemed to be floating above the stage (just as Taglioni appears to be doing in the lithographs of the 1830s) and she managed the difficult feat of making an old-fashioned style seem sincere and natural despite its occasional quaintness.

Yet, whatever her temperamental and physical affinities with the dance of the Romantic age, Evdokimova has also been seen in the late nineteenth-century classics – as Odette-Odile, Aurora and Raymonda – in interpretations which look first to the choreography for inspiration about the heroine's identity and never seek to impose temperamental decoration upon the text. There results a simplicity and directness of performance which can seem deceptively mild until an audience realises with what quiet dignity Evdokimova has performed the choreography.

Away from this traditional repertory, Evdokimova has been seen in an extreme range of ballets – her career is, in this way, diametrically different from that of Haydée, who benefited from the constant supervision and creative guidance of John Cranko. Evdokimova has danced modern works by many different choreographers, but it is in two works by the American Glen Tetley, *Greening* and *Sphinx*, in particular, that she has found roles which match her gallery of Romantic portraits. In *Greening* she portrayed the central female figure caught up in a web of loneliness and longing; as the Sphinx in Tetley's adaptation of Cocteau's *Machine Infernale*, which tells of the encounter between Oedipus and the Sphinx, she showed the inevitability of the Sphinx's quest for death and for Oedipus's love. The contrast between the tense, doomed figure of the Sphinx and that of Bournonville's decorous floating Sylphide suggests something of the range and theatrical vitality of Evdokimova's talent.

If the French proudly regard Yvette Chauviré as a national treasure, *La Chauviré Nationale*, so, too, do the Italians think of their greatest ballerina, Carla Fracci. In a long career, thanks to extended seasons with American Ballet Theatre and thanks also to her untiring work dancing throughout Italy, Fracci has achieved the status of a national heroine of Italian ballet and an international star. After graduating from the ballet school at La Scala, Milan, in 1954. Fracci was quickly identified as a Romantic artist of great charm: in a celebrated performance of Dolin's *Pas de Quatre*, which reproduced Perrot's famous quartet of 1845, three supreme stylists of the Romantic dance – Alicia Markova, Margrethe Schanne and Yvette Chauviré – were joined by the young Fracci who performed wonderfully in the role of that earlier Italian divinity, Fanny Cerrito. In 1960, when she was already prima ballerina of La Scala, Fracci gained her first international success when she danced Giselle in London with Festival Ballet and the expansion of her career thereafter is a story of developing technique and increasing acclaim throughout the world.

It would have been easy for the young Fracci to become trapped in the Romantic repertory for which she seemed so ideally suited by talent and looks. Certainly, *Giselle* and *La Sylphide* were to remain constants throughout her career. Her performances in partnership with Erik Bruhn at American Ballet Theatre during the 1960s created a sensation; there existed such exceptional rapport between the two artists that (as in all great partnerships) the living moment of the drama was made real to performers and to public alike.

Fracci's repertory included, of course, the staple tasks of the ballerina – *The Sleeping Beauty, Swan Lake, Coppélia, La Fille mal gardée*, and versions of *Romeo and Juliet* by Tudor, Cranko and Nureyev. She has also been seen in Italy in a series of works which have been specially created to frame her gifts: stagings of *The Seagull, La Strada* and, in a revival of one of the most celebrated Italian ballets of the last century, *Excelsior*. In more modern choreography, she has also been admired as a passionate and earthy Medea, choreographed by John Butler and partnered by Mikhail Baryshnikov, as Cullberg's Miss Julie, and as Desdemona in Limón's *The Moor's Pavane*. In everything she does, the serenely beautiful Fracci *persona* is an abiding quality. Like every ballerina who personifies a nation's ideals about dancing – Fonteyn at the Royal Ballet; Ulanova at the Bolshoi; Chauviré at the Paris Opéra; Suzanne Farrell at the New York City Ballet – Fracci speaks for Italian dance, for something both gracious and graceful. Her warm temperament and style recall Italian *bel canto* in balletic terms.

The Ballerina and her Partner

The central, culminating moment of nineteenth-century ballets was the *grand pas de deux*, that moment when the ballerina was presented to her public in the dutiful and attentive arms of her partner, the *premier danseur*. But it should not be assumed that these two performers were equal partners. The century had seen the ballerina emerge as the dominant figure in ballet, an ascent to stardom and superiority which began with Marie Taglioni's triumph as the Sylphide in 1832. Male dancers were, as the century progressed, to recede further and further into the background and the ballerina was to claim the limelight as entirely hers in most of the ballets presented in Paris, London and the rest of Europe (the only exception was in Copenhagen, where August Bournonville insisted that there should be in his ballets equality of dance, feeling and technique between men and women). During the Petipa years in Russia the ballets came to centre entirely round the radiant figure of the ballerina. Her image became codified, iconic, as Mikhail Fokine noted with regret in his *Memoirs* when he discussed the ballet at the Mariinsky Theatre as he knew it when he first appeared there as a dancer at the turn of the twentieth century.

'The ballerina interpreted a role on stage: the ballerina, because the ballerina was the most important person in the ballet, and because a dancer who had achieved this title was very proud of her position. She wished it to be clear to everyone, immediately upon her entrance on stage, that she was not just a dancer but the ballerina. In pursuit of acquiring the ballerina look there evolved a special proud stance: a unique habit of holding the head almost immobile, the stretching of the neck, a peculiar gait.'

Thus the ballerina appeared, in tutu and jewels, triumphantly herself. Although certain great artists – Zucchi for one, and later Pavlova – were to suggest that there were emotional and dramatic resonances to the characters that the ballerina played which must be respected, and before which the 'ballerina' nature of the role was unimportant, the majority of Petipa's stagings were intended to display the full resources of a massive company in processions, divertissements and national dances; grandiose and extravagant ensembles which had, at their heart, the image of the ballerina as motive force for the action and the focus of all that was happening on stage. The ballerina was to be displayed, in solos whose ingenuities showed off her gifts with maximum charm and bravura, and then as the heroine of the *pas de deux*. This was the final statement about her importance, the dramatic climax of the work, a sequence where the various threads of the plot might be seen to be tied up and the artistry of the ballerina exhibited through the formulae of the *pas de deux* itself.

Right *Tamara Karsavina and
Vaslav Nijinsky in Mikhail
Fokine's* Le Spectre de la rose.
*Far right Alexandra Danilova and
Frederic Franklin in* Coppélia *as
staged by the Ballet Russe de Monte
Carlo. This ballet was toured round
America by the Ballet Russe with
Danilova and Franklin as its
irresistible stars.*
Previous page *Margot Fonteyn
and Rudolph Nureyev in Frederick
Ashton's* Marguerite and
Armand, *the ballet which provided
the perfect summation of their
partnership.*

After the opening adagio, in which the ballerina was promenaded, lifted and shown off on the strong arms of her cavalier, there ensued a solo for the *danseur,* then a solo for the ballerina in which her special steps might be displayed: finally, the coda when the ballerina's virtuosity – and rather less so, that of her partner – was put on dazzling display in a cascade of fast and brilliant steps. Thus it was ordained by Petipa, and thus it remained for many years and, indeed, remains to this day in certain modern ballets. Of course, there were changes in the format of the *pas de deux*, but it was always the high-point of the action, supposedly celebrating the love of two characters, but more truly seen as an excuse for the ballerina's art to be extended as she was manipulated by the male dancer.

The subservient role of the male is noticeable in most traditional and honest restagings of the old repertory, although *premiers danseurs* today try to share, if not to steal, the ballerina's thunder. It is only in Bournonville's *pas de deux* that we see how the partnership between man and woman on stage could be a true and equal companionship, and not just a vehicle for a star and attendant servant. In Bournonville's *pas de deux* the ballerina is hardly lifted by her partner, as she is in the Petipa repertory. The man and woman dance side by side, the man given as many occasions, and perhaps more, for display than the woman. More usually, however, the supremacy of the ballerina in the nineteenth century meant that partnering was conventional and that the male dancer's chief task was to show off his ballerina with maximum skill to her public. He was, in the convenient term, a *porteur,* and often as uninteresting

to the public as a piece of scenery on which the ballerina could lean. In some iniquitous cases the male dancer was abolished altogether and *danseuses en travesti* partnered the ballerina. This was the fact in certain ballets featuring Fanny Elssler, who was partnered by her sister Thérèse, while in *Coppélia* the role of Frantz, the hero, was taken by the enchantingly pretty Eugénie Fiocre. Although Petipa and Bournonville never accepted this curious state of affairs, it was with the arrival of the Diaghilev Ballet Russe that there began to emerge a new relationship between the ballerina and her partner. In 1911 in *Le Spectre de la Rose* Karsavina and Nijinsky performed as equals.

Even in the traditional nineteenth-century repertory unstated sexual complicity was often implied in the *pas de deux*. It could be a matter of courtship (in the *pas de deux* in Act II of *Swan Lake*), or of seduction (*Swan Lake*, Act III). It could show dawning love (*Giselle*, Act I), and protective love (Act II), or love triumphant and secure (*The Sleeping Beauty*, Act III). In the ballets of the twentieth century there is greater variety and less restraint. In Frederick Ashton's *La Fille mal gardée*, the lovers delight in each other's company in the cornfield *pas de deux*; in MacMillan's *Isadora* sexual pleasure is to be seen, and also the intense grief experienced by Isadora and Paris Singer at the loss of two children. In John Cranko's *The Taming of the Shrew* the *pas de deux* becomes a battle of wits and of temperament; in his *Onegin* the final duet shows the renunciation of love. The range of the *pas de deux* has been extended, but each and every one depends upon the partnership of a ballerina and a male dancer that must encompass physical accord and responsiveness, a spiritual and emotional sympathy, as well as a common understanding of the artistic aims and the dramatic matter to be expressed.

The conventionalities of partnering are taught in ballet school: boys learn early how they must support and hold a girl in what is known in ballet as 'double work'. But this is merely a first introduction to the mechanics of holding and lifting their female partner and of presenting her in the most courteous fashion to the public. There ensues, once a dancer has entered a professional company, a more detailed study which will teach the man how to judge his partner's balances, how to enhance her technical effects in *pirouettes* or in lifts, and how to make her seem both weightless and ideally graceful, even when she is not. It does no harm to remember, when watching a *pas de deux,* that the ballerina being carried so effortlessly by the male dancer is a flesh and blood woman. She may be a featherweight of only six and a half stone but she may weigh over a stone more than this, and she has to be manipulated and carried and transferred about the stage as if her weight were nothing at all. Certain modern 'lifts' require the ballerina to be lifted and held high over the man's head on one arm. The brute strength called for to do this must never be made obvious by the man, and the ballerina for her part can help him by assisting in her lift-off into the air, and by learning how to distribute her weight easily into her partner's arms.

In Soviet ballet, there was a tendency during the 1920s and 1930s towards a far more acrobatic and athletic style of partnership, which has left its mark in the high lifts and throws that are still included in some Russian choreography today. This style of Soviet partnering has been immortalised in two exhibition *pas de deux, Spring Waters* (by Asaf Messerer) and *The Moszkowski Waltz* (by Vassily Vainonen). In both pieces, the ballerina launches herself at her partner in horizontal leaps, to be securely caught in his arms, while in *Spring Waters* the final exit finds the ballerina held high on one outstretched arm of her partner as he races from the stage. The effect is wildly exhilarating, and smacks not a little of kitsch, of a Tarzan and Jane relationship, of gymnastic exercise verging on bad taste. But the sight of two well-rehearsed and magnificently responsive dancers surging over the stage, passionately involved with the dance and with each other, is unfailingly exciting. It also represents a development in Soviet ballet which is discovered in more serious and considerable works of art; in the lifts in Vainonen's version of *The Nutcracker,* in which the Sugar Plum Fairy is thrown through the air by two of her partners, to be caught in the arms of two others; in the high-floating partnering which is part of the second act of *Giselle,* when the Wili Giselle seems to fly and poise herself on Albrecht's upheld arms; and in the high lifts in the ballets of Yuri Grigorovich in which the man carries the heroine joyously above his head in beautiful arcs of movement that clearly communicate the intensity of the lovers' feelings.

Partnering is a true art for a man. Certain male dancers have made impressive contributions to ballet not by reason of any great virtuosity, but because they have

Alicia Markova and Anton Dolin in the second act of Giselle, *a ballet in which their partnership reached its high point. This photograph was taken during the first season of Festival Ballet in 1950.*

Following page *Yekaterina Maximova and Vladimir Vasiliev of the Bolshoi Ballet in the* pas de deux *from* Don Quixote, *to which they brought impeccable style and infectious high spirits.*

demonstrated perfect manners and unerring strength, giving a great feeling of security to their ballerina and showing her to best advantage.

What the ballerina seeks first of all in a partnership is a sense of physical security. The man's arms must be there when they are needed, his support must be unfailing and almost intuitive, so that she becomes in a sense free to dance her best. Many are the occasions when a *pas de deux* has been ruined, both physically and emotionally, because of a lack of sympathy between the partners: the *pirouettes* have been stopped at the wrong moment, the ballerina turned off-centre and held slightly away from her public, and the closing esctatic moment has ended in unease. There are many occasions too when the ballerina has been unceremoniously hoisted into the air, and the male dancer's hands have slipped upwards from her waist to form a stranglehold round her bust, which is as unhelpful to the ballerina as it looks unflattering.

Far more memorable, however, are those moments when the relationship between the ballerina and the *danseur* has seemed so intense that it is as if two bodies are thinking and working as one, when both artists seem to demonstrate a complete faith in and total understanding of each other. Then partnership becomes one of the most exhilarating aspects of dancing, with complete physical trust matched by complete sympathy of feeling and artistic aim.

Such partnerships as that of Alicia Markova and Anton Dolin are rare and are honoured as such. Based on a common background – both were British-born and Russian-trained – theirs was a professional relationship that existed for thirty years. Their talents and temperaments were very different, but mysteriously complementary. Anton Dolin's dignity, his vivid stage personality and the panache of his temperament were the perfect foil for the elegance and classic purity of Alicia Markova, who floated in his arms and found in him an ideally responsive partner. Their shared repertory had an emotional and physical quality that was perfectly balanced.

By contrast, the partnership which united Margot Fonteyn and Rudolf Nureyev came about by chance when she was over forty and he was only twenty-three. Nevertheless, they found in each other's temperaments a means of dramatic communion and physical response which charged their joint performances with an exceptional electricity. Fonteyn was then one of the greatest figures in British ballet. For twenty-five years she had effectively led the Royal Ballet company and her performances in *The Sleeping Beauty* and *Swan Lake*, and in the many ballets created for her by Ashton, made her seem the epitome of the English national style. Her career was entering its final phase when Nureyev, attended with all the brouhaha of his defection in the previous year from the Kirov Ballet while in Paris, appeared on the scene. Their first performance together, in *Giselle* with the Royal Ballet in February 1962, announced that a new theatrical magic had been created.

Fonteyn's delicate, lyric manner, very English in its reserve and classical in its discretion, combined in a wholly unexpected and unlikely way with the fire and ardent youth of the young Russian. Despite its quietness, Fonteyn's temperament was as forceful as Nureyev's in all its turbulence – and his first effect was to galvanise

Fonteyn's dancing and rejuvenate her style. With Nureyev, she began to dance better, more adventurously, even more strongly, a tribute both to her willingness to learn and to her impeccably balanced physique which had always been one of her greatest advantages. The confrontation and accommodation of Nureyev's style with an artist so different, yet so responsive, resulted in a partnership on stage which did, in fact, achieve the rare distinction of seeming a love affair conducted in public. Rehearsal could polish the minutiae of the performance: on stage their combined personalities flared in mutual response and evident affection.

The ideal statement about this partnership was to come, appropriately enough, with a creation: Frederick Ashton's *Marguerite and Armand*. For twenty-five years he had been making ballets which explored and extended Fonteyn's gifts: now he was faced both with the 'new' Fonteyn who was so warmly responsive to Nureyev's presence, and with Nureyev's driving passion as well. The perfect vehicle, the perfect score and the perfect interpreters seemed miraculously to come together in this version of *La Dame aux camélias*, set to Liszt's piano sonata. The racing emotions of the story, the desperate flights of passion and the inevitability of tragedy were all to be heard in the score; and in the performances of the two principals the sweep of feeling, the ardent passion of Armand, the worldly wisdom of Marguerite and her sudden grasping at an improbable happiness, were presented with the most telling theatrical fervour. *Marguerite and Armand* happens to be a good ballet as well as a good vehicle, and it immortalised a partnership with the same sensitivity and same sense of physical inevitability as *Le Spectre de la Rose* did for Karsavina and Nijinsky.

That partnerships can grow from the basis of a common schooling, followed by membership of a parent company with its established repertory as proving ground, is handsomely demonstrated by the artistic collaboration of Antoinette Sibley and Anthony Dowell with the Royal Ballet, as with Yekaterina Maximova and Vladimir Vasiliev with the Bolshoi Ballet (they are also man and wife – partnership can go no further!). With Sibley and Dowell, both graduates of the Royal Ballet School, although four years apart, there was an additional factor: they were first chosen as partners by a choreographer. When Ashton cast them as Titania and Oberon in *The Dream* in 1964, what his choreographic eye saw was a symmetry of physique, a complementary bodily accord that had been enhanced by their common schooling: the two bodies were matched, and putting them together was to produce a cho-reographic coherence, set off by the dramatic tension in the temperamental contrast of the smoothly elegant Dowell and the vividly emotional Sibley. Their dancing in *The Dream*, and thereafter, seemed the apotheosis of the English (which meant Ashtonian) style: fleet, elegant, very musical and very pure in line.

This partnership, once initiated, was to take off and endure, even resuming after Sibley's return to dancing following a lengthy absence due to injury and motherhood. It was a perfectly natural, and ideally responsive, accord between two artists who shared the same dance language, voiced with impeccably English accents. Their physical sympathy was remarkable: line was well matched; musical phrasing was

*Antoinette Sibley and Anthony Dowell in Frederick
Ashton's* Symphonic Variations. *The purity and
harmony in the dancing of these two Royal Ballet
stars epitomised the English style.*

identical – and these mechanics were the product of long hours of rehearsal and the guidance of a notable English *danseur* and teacher (himself Fonteyn's partner for many years), Michael Somes. These sweated hours of practice are essential if a partnership is to allow the artists to express themselves and their joint identity during performance without worrying constantly about the sheer nuts and bolts of the dance. More important still is the unity – that combination of two artists which is greater than the sum of its parts – which Sibley and Dowell possess. The Sibley-Dowell readings of the classics – *The Sleeping Beauty*, *Swan Lake* and *Giselle* – were soon fired by the youthful splendour of their technique and by the classic decorum of their manner. In their earliest full-length roles – Romeo and Juliet – they brought a touching innocence and grace to parts made for very different artists. Then, in 1973, came *Manon*, created for them by MacMillan and celebrating in three acts the mirror-image effect of their dancing: that priceless emotional and almost psychic sympathy in performance which meant that the drama and the dance seemed an inevitable extension of the performers' personalities and feelings.

The partnership of Yekaterina Maximova and Vladimir Vasiliev at the Bolshoi Ballet is in many ways similar to that of Sibley and Dowell. Their training in the Bolshoi School (Maximova is by one year the elder of the two) gave them a basic technical sympathy which is the foundation of their partnership. In ballets such as *Don Quixote*, *Spartacus* and *The Nutcracker*, the combination of perfectly attuned physical bravura and of vivid emotional response won universal and unrestrained acclaim. Theirs was a great theatrical partnership that seemed intuitive in its immediacy and was so polished, technically, as to defeat criticism.

With Marcia Haydée and Richard Cragun of the Stuttgart Ballet we see what is in effect a partnership fostered and shaped by a choreographer. Richard Cragun, born in California, attended the Royal Ballet School; so for a time did Haydée, before she joined the Grand Ballet du Marquis de Cuevas. Cragun joined the Stuttgart Ballet in 1962, shortly after Cranko had appointed Haydée his ballerina. Within three years Cragun was promoted to principal and began dancing in ballets with Haydée. Haydée's special gift of emotional expressivity was already being explored by Cranko – in *Romeo and Juliet* and *Onegin* – and Cragun took over the leading male roles in these ballets as Haydée's partner, beginning that progress towards a complete physical and emotional responsiveness which was soon to be a mark of their dancing together.

It was, it must be added, also the reflection of an off-stage companionship, and in 1969 Cranko made a loving and vastly amusing commentary on their partnership with *The Taming of the Shrew*. Haydée and Cragun gave one of the most beguiling and entertaining displays of double work in modern ballet. The final *pas de deux* was a triumphant assertion of true love between the battling pair. If Haydée's Katherine struck out as viciously as she could at Cragun's Petruchio, and stamped on his feet, Cragun was no less willing to pull Haydée's feet from under her and bring her crashing to the ground. To bring these tricks off required impeccable timing, physical trust and the power to let the choreography speak without allowing the dance to become coarsened or obvious. Split-second timing of physical and emotional effects – one as important as the other – were the result of meticulous rehearsal but also of the common sensitivity of the two partners.

Far left Haydée and Cragun as Katherine and Petruchio in a pas de deux *from John Cranko's* The Taming of the Shrew. *The pose catches the lovers at the final moment when all their battles are over.* Left *Suzanne Farrell and Peter Martins in the* pas de deux *from Balanchine's* Apollo. *Here is the quintessential New York City Ballet style of our time.*

Carla Fracci and Erik Bruhn in the first act of Giselle *with American Ballet Theatre in the 1960s.*

Of modern American partnerships, one is pre-eminent: that of New York City Ballet's Suzanne Farrell with Peter Martins (now joint chief ballet master of the company). Suzanne Farrell had been for several years a favourite dancer of George Balanchine, and her art seemed for many people to sum up a great deal about the style and attitudes of the New York City Ballet in matters of speed and clarity of execution, and even of physique. Peter Martins, a product of the Royal Danish Ballet and of its Bournonville schooling, was very different in every artistic way except one: he is tall, as is Farrell, and, as he explained in his book of memoirs, *Far from Denmark*, 'The reason I was invited to join New York City Ballet was that I made a good partner for her.' He went on to note that Balanchine did not encourage steady partnerships – in the copious output of his choreography, the very fact of a 'permanent' partnership would seem inhibiting if he was obliged constantly to consider two artists as inseparable. But there was an immediate physical sympathy between himself and Farrell: 'I'm tall and so is Suzanne, and we both dance with spacious, ample movement and gestures. We believe in the pressure of performance, that what happens, happens before an audience. Suzanne is a dancer who likes to take risks, to surprise an audience, to highlight the unexpected, and to dance with a seemingly spontaneous reaction to the music ... As a partner, I have to watch her with a different kind of concentration than I need for other dancers, for she is totally unpredictable, and sometimes her performances veer towards the eccentric and fantastic. She has been quoted as saying that she likes to challenge me, and I do feel that challenge.'

These comments, from a dancer who has partnered many ballerinas in a wide-ranging repertory, are evidence of a partnership that has been built upon the respect and trust between two artists in a company where the male dancer has in the past often had a subservient role. Thus, despite the modernity of the repertory, there is implicit in Martins's comments the 'traditional' view of the *danseur* as attendant upon the ballerina. But this being the New York City Ballet, and the artists being involved in choreography by Balanchine and Robbins, there resulted a far from conventional partnership. Suzanne Farrell's dancing has a quality of daring which speaks through her virtuosity and acuteness of musical understanding: Peter Martins's monumental power, his physical dignity and size of movement, seemed at times to be a foil to Farrell's dancing and also a necessary response to it: their styles were complementary, fitting together in a union that was as much emotional and aesthetic as dynamic. In the Diamonds section from Balanchine's *Jewels*, a tribute to the world of Petipa, they became the reincarnation of a Mariinsky ballerina and *premier danseur*; in Balanchine's choreography to Ravel's *Tzigane*, Farrell's dancing seemed the visual realization of the wild cadenzas of the violin writing, as she twined around Martins, supported by his strength; and in the ravishing Balanchine/Gluck *Chaconne*, an Elysian view of the pair, sublimely matched, sublimely involved in dancing, was created which spoke of the beauty of their joint art and of the beauty of the dance itself. *Chaconne* remains one of the great and unassailable statements about a man and woman dancing together in the twentieth century.

Ballerina Roles

There are certain roles in the traditional ballet repertory which are still commonly considered to provide the yardsticks of the ballerina's art, as they also proclaim the status of the company which presents them. Just as great singers anticipate that they will be tested against the demands of the operas of Bellini and Donizetti, Verdi and Puccini, so ballerinas and aspirant dancers in the major classical companies anticipate that they will in time be faced with the challenges of *La Sylphide* and *Giselle*, *Coppélia* and *Swan Lake*, *Raymonda* and *The Sleeping Beauty*, *La Bayadère* and *The Nutcracker*. These are the precious heritage of the nineteenth-century classic dance: each makes specific and exact demands upon the art of the dancer (as upon the artistry of the company that stages it) and each can still live as a vital theatrical experience for audiences if it is conscientiously staged and performed with proper love and understanding. One such challenging ballet is *La Sylphide*, presented at the Paris Opéra in 1832. It was created by Filippo Taglioni for his daughter Marie, and so strong has been the impact of Taglioni's dancing, and her style, that even today ballerinas seek to emulate those qualities of lightness and grace, of demure charm and feathery skill, which were hers.

The action of the ballet was inspired by a novel of the 1820s by Charles Nodier, *Trilby or the Elf of Argyle,* which dealt with a Scottish lass who was lured away from her home by a male sprite. With the sexual roles reversed, there emerged the story of the young crofter, James, who is visited by a Sylphide who loves him. James is betrothed to Effie, but the attraction of the Sylphide's otherworldly beauty and charm is too much for him. At the end of the ballet's first act, he flees from his home with the Sylphide, leaving Effie disconsolate. In the second act, James and the Sylphide are now in the sprite's natural habitat of a mountain glen. Here James tries to possess the Sylphide. A wicked witch, Madge, whom he has offended, plots his downfall and that of the Sylphide by offering James a poisoned scarf – telling him only that if he will but wind it round the Sylphide's arms, she will be his for ever.

This James contrives to do, and the Sylphide's wings drop off as she loses her immortality and dies. She is borne away by her sister sylphs, while James is left alone. He watches his erstwhile fiancée, Effie, going to her wedding with his rival, Gurn. At the final curtain, James falls to the ground with Madge standing over him, cursing and triumphant.

The narrative deals with one of the central themes of art in the European Romantic age: that of the lure of an exotic and otherworldly love, of the plight of the Romantic hero who, in pursuit of an impossible passion, finds himself cut off from the real world, and by pursuing a dream brings about his own downfall. The role of the Sylphide identified the ballerina with a gauzy and immaterial style, floating and drifting across the stage, gently beautiful, diaphanous and enchanting, dreamlike and, in Marie Taglioni's performance, poised on the very tips of her toes as if fleeing from the constraints of the earth. The ballerina was an idealised being, caught up in a drama of feverish emotions.

It is ironic that *La Sylphide* survives in a version that was staged despite its choreographer's mistrust of just these emotions. August Bournonville, as we have mentioned, mounted *La Sylphide* for his pupil Lucile Grahn because he wished her to be moulded in the manner of Taglioni, in spite of his dislike of the moral ambiguities of the role. Yet in Paris the ballet was to disappear from the repertory after thirty years and, although Petipa revived and revised it in St Petersburg, it was

Right Roland Petit as James supports Nina Vyroubova in the second act of Victor Gsovsky's recreation of La Sylphide *for the Ballets des Champs Elysées. Vryoubova was a touching and exquisite sylph, a worthy incarnation of the role.*
Previous page Alicia Markova as the Wili Giselle, at the moment when she first appears from the grave.

only to know continual performance in Copenhagen with the Royal Danish Ballet. Because of the relative isolation of the company, the work was kept alive through the continuity of performance by succeeding generations of ballerinas, albeit with certain changes and emendations in text and dance style that were inevitable over a period of more than one hundred years. Nevertheless, film showing Danish dancers performing fragments of the choreography in 1906 suggests that since that date little change has been effected in the choreography itself, although dancers' physiques have altered and styles of execution of the steps are somewhat (although not much) different.

Thus it is the Bournonville *La Sylphide* which provides us with one of the most precious insights into the dance of the Romantic age. The challenge for ballerinas is to make the role of the Sylphide live, both by attempting the 're-creation' of a style and by presenting a view of this touching drama that is credible and attractive for

*Eva Evdokimova as the Sylphide in the first act of
the Royal Danish Ballet's production of the ballet.*

Fracci's Sylphide, enchanted by the poisoned scarf. James is danced here by Erik Bruhn.

audiences today. Plainly, lightness and a gentle charm are among the first requisites for an artist assuming the wings and flowered chaplet of the Sylphide (and this is true, too, for those ballerinas who have appeared in versions other than Bournonville's: in the re-stagings by Victor Gsovsky for the Ballets des Champs-Elysées in 1946 and by Pierre Lacotte for the Paris Opéra in 1972, both sought to restore something of the version danced by Marie Taglioni).

It is part of the domesticity of the Bournonville style for women that nothing must seem extravagant or be contaminated with virtuoso technical effects. Instead, buoyancy and aerial grace inform the choreography. The Sylphide is often childlike and innocent in her ways, but as she skims and flies over the stage her dancing is supported by the technical security that a ballerina must have. The playful and ethereal nature of the role suddenly changes, however, when the poisoned scarf is placed over

the Sylphide's shoulders. At that moment the ballerina must suggest the tragedy of her plight, as death starts to claim her and she returns James's wedding ring to him before she is carried away by her sister sylphs. It is a pathetic, rather than deeply tragic, moment and must be kept within the stylistic bounds of the rest of the ballet: the Sylphide leaves the world as gently as she has danced in it.

On the morning after the first night of *Giselle* at the Paris Opéra on 28 June 1841, the composer of its score, Adolphe Adam, wrote a letter to the librettist, Vernoy de St Georges. He noted that *Giselle* 'was born last night and her delivery was accomplished by circumstances that give promise of a long life ... Our success has been most magnificent; the first act, which is the weaker of the two, had already achieved a success, thanks to Carlotta who was ravishing in it; when the second act came ... it transformed a success into a triumph.'

In discussing Carlotta Grisi we have already touched on the creation of this best-known of the ballets of the Romantic age. What captivated contemporary audiences was the intensity of the drama, the way in which the work displayed the double nature of balletic Romanticism in a single evening, contrasting the rustic charm and quaintness and the sparkling dances of the medieval Thuringian scene with the nocturnal mystery, the moonlit outpourings of feeling and the airy flights of the forest scene in the second act.

Far left *Margrethe Schanne as the Sylphide with Poul Gnatt as James. Schanne was the greatest Danish Sylphide of her generation.*
Left *Galina Ulanova as Giselle with Nikolay Fadeyechev as Albrecht in the second act of* Giselle *as danced by the Bolshoi Ballet at Covent Garden in 1956.*

The first act is of this world: Giselle, betrayed in her love for the disguised Count Albrecht, dies of a broken heart when she discovers that he is already betrothed to the Duke of Courland's daughter. In the second act, set by Giselle's grave in a forest, the ghostly night-dancers – the Wilis – assemble. Giselle's spirit emerges from her tomb to be initiated into their rites and to learn that any man who ventures into their power must be danced to death. Albrecht comes to lay flowers on Giselle's grave, is caught by the Wilis, and forced to dance. Giselle is torn between her nature as a Wili, eager for his death, and an abiding love for him: she becomes a protective force, trying to shield him from the vengeance of the Queen of the Wilis, Myrtha, and sustains him as he dances by dancing with him. Just as his collapse and death seem imminent, dawn breaks and the Wilis' power is broken by the sun's rays: Giselle's love has survived the grave and has saved the man she loved, even though this love had proved fatal for her.

When *Giselle* disappeared from the Paris Opéra repertory in the 1860s, it was already securely rooted in the Russian repertory. The first St Petersburg staging was a pirated one, produced in 1842 by Antoine Titus, a ballet master who had gone to Paris to see the work and then returned to mount his own version. But when Jules Perrot arrived in St Petersburg as first ballet master, he made his own production, designed to show off Carlotta Grisi and Fanny Elssler, the great dramatic interpreters of the role, during their visits to St Petersburg. The staging was later revised by

Far left *Yvette Chauviré as Giselle in the second act of the ballet as staged by the Paris Opera in 1958.*
Left *Natalia Bessmertnova's portrayal of Giselle's mad scene.*
Below *Margot Fonteyn as Giselle and Rudolf Nureyev as Albrecht, during the dance of destruction ordered by the Queen of the Wilis. It was in this ballet that the celebrated partnership of Fonteyn and Nureyev began at Covent Garden in February 1962.*

Marius Petipa, but throughout its unbroken history in Russia the piece has always been revered as a touching drama which contains in the central role one of the greatest challenges to a ballerina's art. We have noted how such ballerinas as Pavlova, Karsavina and Spessivtseva, and later Ulanova, were to succeed in it and how, through Markova's presence in London, it was acquired by the infant Royal Ballet in 1934 to become part of the British ballet-goer's heritage. It first returned to the Paris Opéra repertory in 1924, staged for Spessivtseva; later Serge Lifar produced the work, giving a stronger emphasis to the role of Albrecht but also inviting celebrated ballerinas – Semyonova and Spessivtseva – to dance it, and encouraging French ballerinas to return to a role which was part of their birthright. Thus Yvette Chauviré, one of the greatest Giselles, was able to illuminate the role, and subsequently ballerinas of the Opéra – Lycette Darsonval, Noella Pontois and Elisabeth Platel – have been justly admired for their interpretations.

The appeal of Giselle as a role is implicit in the dichotomy between the two acts: the ballerina has the chance to play a simple peasant girl and then to reach the pinnacle of the first act with a mad scene of exceptional pathos; in the second act the weightless, compassionate girl who dances for and with Albrecht is able to deploy all the power of pure and beautiful technique in choreography that calls for an imponderable grace and also a saturated sense of emotion as the drama (quite as intense as in the first act) unfolds. The problems of the role are also connected with this dichotomy: the ballerina must reconcile the peasant girl and the wraith, she must suggest the quality of Giselle's love in the first act and show it transformed and transmuted into something unearthly and pure in the second act.

Natalia Makarova, the greatest Giselle of our time, resolved this problem after nearly twenty years of dancing the role: in her *Dance Autobiography* she noted: 'Both acts of *Giselle* are manifestations of her soul, her inner states of being. And her soul is one. In the first act, still in her corporeal existence, she lives with ordinary human concerns – the dances with the villagers, the suitor, Hilarion, the meeting with the Count and with Bathilde, the unmasking of Albrecht, her madness – which are transformed in her by the first feelings of love. But freedom from these wearying realities comes with death. In the second act, her soul, freed of all that is worldly, superficial and ordinary, is filled with regal quietude and wisdom, and she becomes a bearer of eternal femininity, of chastity and purity. And in the purity she is not capable of punishing; she is now above the earthly passions and their excitements. Only forgiveness is available to her, and it comes from her naturally, from her deep feminine sympathy. Having acquired this angle of vision, I could assimilate the entire role ... Now, for me, there is no break between the first and second acts – the first leads into the second.'

These words suggest something of the richness of insight that a great artist will bring to a ballet, and will – we trust – pass on to her successors. They illustrate, too, the degree of dedication with which the ballerina has to approach her work. Such emotional insights are, necessarily, allied to physical insights, ways of encompassing the steps to give them their maximum beauty and emotional and dramatic effect. To be able to dance Giselle, in the first instance, implies a physical suitability for the role; ideally, a delicacy of physique and a clarity of technique especially suited to the image of the wraith in the second act. Few are the ballerinas who have this actual physical equipment, but the great Giselles are those in whom body and spirit seem to find an accord, and who communicate the life of the role with a force that makes the hallowed Romantic drama seem alive and infinitely touching.

It is one of the mysteries of ballet that *Coppélia*, a work blessed with a superlative score and, in many productions, with superior choreography (George Balanchine has made his own version for New York City Ballet; Petipa made the first Russian staging that was seen in St Petersburg in 1884), should so often today be considered only suitable for children and be dismissed as somehow inferior — because light-hearted — to more pretentious works, which are thought to be 'tragic' and therefore 'important'. *Coppélia* is, or can be when lovingly treated, a comic masterpiece that offers a ballerina one of the most enchanting roles in the repertory. Like every comedy, it needs to be produced with complete seriousness and to be performed with the seriousness of intention with which *The Sleeping Beauty* should be danced. Comedy in the theatre is notoriously harder to bring off than tragedy, and the number of outstanding Swanildas is, in our experience, fewer than the outstanding interpreters of Odette-Odile in *Swan Lake*.

We have discussed *Coppélia*'s early history in writing about the tragedy of Giuseppina Bozzacchi. The original production was maintained in Paris for many years — a succession of French and Italian ballerinas shone in it; it was introduced to Russia first in 1882 in a staging in Moscow by a Belgian choreographer, Joseph Hansen, who had studied (and copied) much of the original Paris staging by St Léon. But many Western stagings owe their origins to the version produced by Marius Petipa in St Petersburg in 1884 and revised by him and Enrico Cecchetti ten years later.

The ballet's theme is adapted in a somewhat vulgarised form from a tale by the German Romantic writer, E. T. A. Hoffmann, and its theme is essentially very moral, seeking to show how a girl must fight for the young man she loves, coming into contact with a form of alchemy in the process, while Frantz's story concerns the temporary rejection of his true love in favour of a mysterious automaton and his eventual realisation of how he has been bewitched. Tragedy also marks the character of Dr Coppélius, for he is seeking to create life, and one of the most beautiful and touching moments in the score is that passage when Coppélius believes that the supposed Coppélia has come to life and has a human soul. (Swanilda's heartless behaviour in tricking the old man may be put down to her willingness to rescue Frantz from what she believes to be danger.)

These may seem subliminal themes to what is, after all, a sunny masterpiece, but ballerinas and producers must be aware of them, and the artificiality of the balletic

Marion Tait as Swanilda impersonating the doll Coppélia and John Auld as Dr Coppélius.

action – with its merry peasants and its comic businesss – must not wholly destroy the more serious overtones of the narrative. The ballet's action is simply stated: in the first act, set in a Galician village, we find Swanilda in love with Frantz, whose feelings for her are less than sincere – he has fallen under the spell of a mysterious girl whom he has seen seated on the balcony of the house of Dr Coppélius, an eccentric old scientist who lives in the village. One evening when Coppélius has gone to the

Alexandra Danilova in a staging of Coppélia *by the Ballet Russe de Monte Carlo*

inn for a drink, Frantz climbs into his house in search of the unknown beauty, while at the same time Swanilda and her friends have also crept surreptitiously into the house in order to discover exactly what Coppélius has been doing.

The second act takes place in Coppélius's workshop, where the girls discover that he manufactures automata. Coppélius returns and chases them away, save for Swanilda who has found the mysterious young woman who has caught Frantz's roving eye. To Swanilda's amazement, she finds that the girl is an automaton, Coppélia, and she takes the doll's place when Coppélius returns to the workshop. No sooner does the old scientist believe that he is alone, than Frantz breaks into the room. Coppélius succeeds in drugging him and attempts to transfer the life force from Frantz into the supposed Coppélia (who is now Swanilda, in disguise). To his joy, the experiment seems to work, for Swanilda plays up to him, but soon she runs wild, seeks to rouse Frantz, and creates havoc with the other dolls. As the act ends, she wakes Frantz up and reveals to Coppélius the trick she has played upon him. As the curtain falls, the old scientist, his doll Coppélia in his arms, weeps at the destruction of his dreams. In

Nadia Nerina as Lise in La Fille mal gardée, *the role created for her in Frederick Ashton's version of the old ballet.*

the third act, a divertissement, the villagers assemble to celebrate the betrothal of various young couples, including Swanilda and Frantz, and Coppélius is recompensed for the damage to his workshop with a gift of money.

What has guaranteed *Coppélia* its continuing place in the repertory is, of course, the miraculous Delibes score, so melodious, so vivid, so alive with charm and energy and wit. It is these qualities which also must be found in the interpreter of the role of Swanilda. The ballerina has, in a sense, to overcome the less attractive side of the character, and to charm an audience into accepting her thoughtless high spirits and her determination to keep Frantz's love. This combination of serious intentions and merriment, of sincerity and madcap high spirits, can prove irresistible when a ballerina contrives the right balance of feeling and humour. The role is ideal for ballerinas with bright *demi-caractère* technique – the ideal soubrette performer who can sparkle through the dances and who possesses that small physique with quick, vivid muscular style which allows for brilliant beaten steps and *pirouettes*.

But it is also a role which suits some classic artists who have all the more usual

qualities of line and nobility of style. Thus Pamela May and Svetlana Beriosova with the Royal Ballet, both of whom are more usually associated with Odette-Odile and Aurora, were enchanting, memorable Swanildas, and Patricia MacBride of New York City Ballet has also danced it successfully although she, too, is associated with more formal ballerina roles. And, as we have mentioned, Alexandra Danilova – a great classic ballerina – was the supreme Swanilda for audiences, both in America and Europe, who fell under the spell of her bewitching sense of humour.

As a pendant to Swanilda, we should add the role of Lise in *La Fille mal gardée* – especially in Ashton's version of the old ballet, created in 1960 for the Royal Ballet at Covent Garden. From its very first performance in Bordeaux in 1789 the ballet had beguiled audiences and, in various versions, with differing scores and choreography, it was performed throughout the nineteenth century, remaining constantly in the Russian/Soviet repertory. But Ashton's version was brand new, with the old Hérold score much edited and improved; it was, from its first performance, clearly a masterpiece of sunlit pastoral humour and enchanting emotion. Lise and Colas were roles conceived for brilliant dancers – Nadia Nerina and David Blair – while the two humorous roles of the Widow Simone and the simpleton Alain were taken by two grand comedy dancers, Stanley Holden and Alexander Grant. Everything about the ballet – its sense of humour as well as its strong narrative, the pretty way Lise fights to keep the young man she loves despite her mother's precautions, the abundant and dazzling dances and the tenderness of the love duets – announced that Swanilda had found in Lise a worthy companion in the twentieth-century repertory.

The most popular of the nineteenth-century classics is *Swan Lake*, the work which every ballet company knows will sell out a theatre, no matter what the quality of the performance or the staging. It enshrines many of the most hallowed clichés about ballet – and has, indeed, imposed its own clichés upon the viewing public worldwide: music by Tchaikovsky, white tutus, girls who are supposed to be swans, and a romantic tale of doomed love. It has also generally received interpretations which are wholly inadequate: the great Odette-Odiles are very few and far between. There are, of course, no absolutes about interpretation. The one absolute about the staging, we believe, is that a traditional presentation based on the version mounted by Petipa and Ivanov at the Mariinsky Theatre in 1894–5 is probably the best and most sympathetic to watch.

The first and most obvious comment must be concerned with sheer technique: the ballerina needs a beautiful line for Odette, and must have the virtuosity necessary for the challenge of the *pas de deux* in the third act, which culminates in the notorious thirty-two *fouettés*. These were interpolated by Petipa to show off the trick-step of Pierina Legnani, the first Odette-Odile at the Mariinsky Theatre. The entire Black Swan duet (a name given to it because in many productions during the past half a century Odile is dressed in black) makes extreme technical demands upon the ballerina and these *fouettés* come as a final test of bravura skill.

Fouettés are a physical knack, and can be taught by a sufficiently skilled teacher, but for many ballerinas they represent a daunting end to the *pas de deux* and frequent are the occasions when they are fudged or incompletely given. Many ballerinas, alas, have insufficient control to perform the step on one spot, as is the strict requirement, and the sight of an Odile gradually travelling over the stage as the *fouettés* grind inexorably on is more usual than the view of the ballerina spinning dazzling on the same spot. Even though audiences have come to expect them, it is better for a ballerina to provide an alternative sequence of steps rather than to increase her own nervous tension by knowing that a difficult *pas de deux* must end with a forbidding and nerve-wracking test of her skill in which she can fail. Some ballerinas have provided alternative sequences; some disdain the *fouettés* – it is recorded that Maya Plisetskaya did not perform them at her New York début as Odile with the Bolshoi Ballet but, to show that the step was mere child's play to her, produced a myriad of impeccable *fouettés* at a later performance. Nadia Nerina, in a performance with the Royal Ballet, once decided justifiably to show off, and substituted thirty-two *entrechats six* – an even more difficult feat – as a response to the challenge of a male dancer who had performed sixteen *entrechats six* as Albrecht in *Giselle* and had thereby created a furore.

But as important as the ballerina's mechanical ability to perform the role is the more serious matter of her understanding of its emotional significance. Ballerinas vary from 'hot' to 'cold' in temperament, and we have rejoiced in interpretations by performers who have seemed both 'icy' and emotionally tempestuous, because their view of the double role has given the ballet a clear dramatic sense. Fonteyn imbued her characterisation with a purity and a grand simplicity that were the fruit of her many years of experience – every great ballerina finds a way of paring away excess from her interpretations so that, as she grows older, they become more pure and concentrated in feeling. Makarova's Odette was a portrait of intense emotion; the great adagio in the second act poured out in a long cantilena of feeling and beautiful 'line'. She imbued the second act with the deepest feelings of tragedy, as Odette found in Siegfried a hope of release from evil enchantment, while her Odile was given with such malevolent brilliance that no Siegfried could resist her. Another Soviet ballerina, Natalia Bessmertnova, has shown how by the very grandeur of her style a great artist may justify the role of Odette-Odile. Because her dancing is so lucid, so clear in tone and so truthful in setting out the choreography, Bessmertnova's Odette-Odile has a poetic dignity that makes the tragedy exceptionally touching.

The key to *Swan Lake*, as to *Giselle*, can be found in the second act where Odette meets Siegfried at the lakeside and his immediate love for her seems to promise her release from the enchanter's spell. To convey both the beauty of the dance and the intensity of the drama requires what Makarova has called the 'singing' lines of the arms as well as great flexibility of the body. These respond to the intense emotionalism of Tchaikovsky's score, music 'in which – or beyond which – one dances. It leads you; it subordinates you to itself; it is almost beyond the ability of the body, as it makes each note concrete, to compete with it. *Swan Lake* has survived the test of

*Far left Natalia Makarova
and Anthony Dowell in the
second-act adagio from* Swan
Lake.
Left Svetland Beriosova as
Odile with the Royal Ballet.

time because the choreography of the ballet frequently rises to the level of the genius of Tchaikovsky's music – especially Ivanov's second act, an absolute masterpiece.' So Makarova describes the challenges and the attraction of the ballet in her *Dance Autobiography*, and it is this combination of musical feeling with a desire to show the audience that feeling through the aspirations of the body which marks the real interpretations of Odette–Odile.

The Sleeping Beauty is the final grand and tremendous vision of the classic dance in the nineteenth century. First staged in St Petersburg in 1890, the ballet is, we believe, a supreme masterpiece with a score that is arguably Tchaikovsky's finest musical attainment, and choreography by Marius Petipa that is the culminating achievement of his career; in Makarova's words 'a triumph of academic virtuosity'.

The role of Aurora is the supreme challenge for the pure classical ballerina. It calls for little or no acting, beyond the presentation to the public of a charming young princess in the first act; a radiant vision in the second; and the ballerina in glorious command of all her gifts in the third act, in the wedding *pas de deux*. Of drama, psychological subtlety, even of characterisation, there is little or no trace. Instead, the ballerina must sustain the narrative thread, and hold her audience across three demanding acts, by the sheer beauty and exquisite force of her dance skill. And it is a style which must meet the most rigorous demands of the classic dance: where, in *Giselle*, the ballerina can seek to suggest the gentle and airy style of Romanticism;

Right *Gelsey Kirkland as Aurora partnered by Stephen Jefferies as Prince Florimund in the third-act* pas de deux. *This photograph commemorates Kirkland's exceptional début in* The Sleeping Beauty *at Covent Garden in 1986.* Centre *Antoinette Sibley as Aurora with the Royal Ballet in a production, with designs by Lila de Nobili, that was staged at the Royal Opera House in 1968. The joyous elegance of Sibley's wonderful interpretation is very clear from this action photograph. She was the greatest Aurora of her generation.* Far right *Margot Fonteyn as Aurora being held by David Blair in one of the fish dives in the third-act* pas de deux.

where in *Swan Lake* she must present the vibrant tragedy of Odette in long, singing lines of movement and then, as Odile, glitter with demonic force to dazzle Siegfried with her technical bravura; as Aurora she has to be constantly aware of the severest laws of classical academic dancing and also know that she cannot find any other help for her performance in dramatics or in emotion. The choreography is the thing, and the only thing she can rely on. Hence Aurora demands a pure and academically proper style, a physique that is very clear and beautifully correct in proportion and a style that is the equivalent of the most beautiful speaking of verse: the 'voice' of the body of an Aurora must be beautiful – she must speak Petipa's alexandrines with ease and clarity of diction.

The great Auroras in our experience have inevitably come from companies and schools where there is a strong tradition of academic training – Leningrad, Paris and London – and this is the basis for the way in which each great ballerina will approach the role, giving it her especial personal stamp even within the rigorous outlines of the way the choreography must be performed. The great interpretations – Fonteyn's with its musicality and its perfect harmony of form, with nothing excessive or strained; the exhilaration of Nerina's coming on stage, as she herself said, like a burst of sunshine; as well as the amazing lightness and astounding clarity of Kolpakova's Aurora with the Kirov Ballet, the sense of youthful grace and serenity of Elisabeth Platel as guest with the Royal Ballet, and the classic grandeur and charm of Ludmila Semenyaka with the Bolshoi Ballet – these were each very different from one another,

yet all were the more glorious because they remained within the most severe and demanding canons of the classic academic style.

With the role of the heroine in Petipa's last masterpiece, *Raymonda*, of 1898, we again find a part which does not offer much dramatic opportunity, but instead must live and convince audiences today by reason of the classic beauty and purity of the ballerina's style. There is a certain difference with Aurora in that, in the last act of *Raymonda*, the scene is set as a Hungarian divertissement (the reason for this, in a work set in medieval Provence with Saracens and Crusaders, is part of the general idiocy of the ballet's narrative). Raymonda is given a Hungarian solo, and in this the ballerina can delightfully suggest the charm and fire of national attitudes. But otherwise the ballet's action remains as a framework, variously bizarre, for the sparkle and brilliance of a ballerina wholly mistress of her art.

In the stagings mounted in Leningrad and Moscow, and in Rudolf Nureyev's production for the Paris Opéra Ballet, we are given the opportunity to admire the technical assurance and the classic distinction of several ballerinas, notably of Irina Kolpakova as a marvellously elegant Raymonda with the Kirov Ballet, and of Ludmila Semenyaka in an interpretation which we find without flaw with the Bolshoi Ballet. Similarly, with the Paris Opéra both Noella Pontois and Elisabeth Platel have given interpretations of exceptional beauty: Pontois displaying qualities of *chic* that seem essentially French in their suggestion of physical wit and sense of style, and Platel

Ludmila Semenyaka rehearsing the first act of Raymonda *in London with the Bolshoi Ballet in 1986 – a picture that conveys exactly the superlative harmony and classic distinction of Semenyaka's peerless performance.*

revealing a beauty, a clarity and incisive precision of dancing that give the choreography an exceptional brilliance of facet, like the finest diamond superlatively cut.

The Nutcracker remains a ballet of constant popularity thanks to its wonderful score, but one which few companies know how to present with anything like proper respect. In it, the ballerina role is, essentially, reduced to nothing but one *pas de deux*, although this is a beautiful duet by Lev Ivanov that demands – and all too rarely receives – a performance from its ballerina of exquisite lightness and charm. The Sugar Plum Fairy's greatest interpreters – Markova with Festival Ballet, Kolpakova with the Kirov Ballet – have been prima ballerinas of elegance and delicacy of phrasing: in the Kirov Ballet (with choreography by Vainonen) the ballerina is thrown high in the air between her four partners and Kolpakova's imponderable manner made this seem entirely credible. No such acrobatics are to be found in the original Ivanov choreography which Markova danced with a clarity and a spun-sugar airiness that no subsequent interpreter has ever been able to match.

The role of Nikiya, whose tragedy is the story of *La Bayadère,* was created by Petipa in St Petersburg in 1877 for his favoured ballerina, Yekaterina Vazem. The action of the ballet, which is set in a legendary India, tells in the first act of a warrior, Solor, who loves Nikiya, a temple dancer (a *bayadère*). They swear their love over the sacred flame of a temple fire, but Nikiya is also loved by the chief Brahmin of the temple in which she dances, and he vows that he will win her. In the second act, the action

Alicia Markova as the Sugar Plum Fairy in The Nutcracker, *an interpretation unrivalled for its delicacy.*

Left *Alla Shelest as Nikiya in* La Bayadère *as staged by the Kirov Ballet in Leningrad.*
Below *Margot Fonteyn as Nikiya and Rudolf Nureyev as Solor in Nureyev's staging of the Kingdom of Shades scene for the Royal Ballet.*

moves to the palace of a Rajah whose daughter is the beautiful Gamzatti. The Rajah has decided that Solor shall marry Gamzatti. When the couple meet, Solor falls under Gamzatti's spell. The Brahmin warns the Rajah and Gamzatti that Solor loves Nikiya and, when Nikiya is summoned to the palace to dance, there is a celebrated dramatic interview between the two women, in which the Princess points out that she can offer Solor wealth and position. The impassioned Nikiya seizes a dagger and is tempted for an instant to stab her rival, but flees from the palace in horror at the thought of her intended action. In the third act the betrothal of Gamzatti and Solor is celebrated in a great festival at which Nikiya must dance. As she performs she is presented with a basket of flowers. She believes them to be from Solor, but they have been procured by Gamzatti and contain a poisonous snake which bites Nikiya. The chief Brahmin offers an antidote to the snake-bite if Nikiya will be his, but she refuses and dies.

The distraught Solor takes opium and dreams, in the fourth act, that he has descended to the Kingdom of the Shades where he sees the ghosts of dead *bayadères* and meets the forgiving shade of Nikiya with whom he dances. It is this act, a grand set-piece of pure classic dancing, which has been staged in the West – although Makarova has also produced the entire ballet for American Ballet Theatre. Soviet stagings of the ballet end at this point, omitting Petipa's fifth act, but in her production Makarova has restored the final scene in which Gamzatti and Solor are to be married by the chief Brahmin in the temple. As they prepare for the wedding, the ghost of Nikiya appears, and the gods avenge her death by destroying the temple, killing all its inhabitants, and allowing Solor to be reunited with Nikiya in an after-life.

For most Western audiences the Shades scene has become well-known since the Kirov Ballet introduced it to London in 1961. Several companies – including the Royal Ballet, the Paris Opéra Ballet, American Ballet Theatre and the National Ballet of Canada – have staged it, and their public has learned to appreciate the immense technical demands of the role of Nikiya. The part offers a combination of Romantic spirituality (rather like that of Giselle in the second act of her ballet) and classic rigour: the ballerina is faced with choreography by Petipa that is both immensely demanding and exquisitely precise. As she deploys the purity of her line and the academic grandeur of her style in the solos and duet, she must also suggest the spiritual quality of Nikiya's existence and her compassionate feelings for Solor. *La Bayadère* is a ballet which offers exceptional challenges to its ballerina: these are requirements of lightness and of almost luminous grace and beauty, which are rarely met. However, Makarova herself, and the *étoile* of the Paris Opéra Ballet, Elisabeth Platel, as well as generations of Leningrad ballerinas – notably Spessivtseva and Kolpakova – have shown the possibilities of the part as one of the great test pieces of a ballerina's artistry and bravura elegance.

Picture Credits

Page 8 SOCIETY FOR CULTURAL RELATIONS WITH THE USSR; page 10 NINA ALAVERT; page 12 ZOE DOMINIC; page 14 DINA MAKAROVA/BBC; page 16 VICTORIA & ALBERT MUSEUM; page 19 (left) MARY EVANS PICTURE LIBRARY; page 19 (right) BULLOZ; page 23 VICTORIA & ALBERT MUSEUM; page 26 PARMENIA MIGEL EKSTROM, NEW YORK; page 28 VICTORIA & ALBERT MUSEUM; page 31 BULLOZ; page 33 CLARKE-CRISP COLLECTION; page 35 (top & bottom) VICTORIA & ALBERT MUSEUM; page 39 (top) CLARKE-CRISP COLLECTION; page 39 (bottom) COLLECTION VIOLLET; page 41 VICTORIA & ALBERT MUSEUM; page 44 HARVARD THEATRE COLLECTION; page 46 HARLINGUE-VIOLLET; page 48 BIBLIOTHEQUE NATIONALE, PARIS; page 50 SABINE YI; page 51 IVOR GUEST COLLECTION; pages 52 & 54 (left) BIBLIOTHEQUE NATIONALE, PARIS; pages 54 (right), 55 & 57 (top) IVOR GUEST COLLECTION; page 57 (bottom) VICTORIA & ALBERT MUSEUM; page 60 CLARKE-CRISP COLLECTION; page 62 (left) BIBLIOTHEQUE NATIONALE, PARIS; page 62 (right) IVOR GUEST COLLECTION; page 63 BIBLIOTHEQUE NATIONALE, PARIS; pages 64, 65 & 66 MUSEUM OF LONDON; page 69 BBC HULTON PICTURE LIBRARY; page 72 BALLET RAMBERT ARCHIVES; page 74 CLARKE-CRISP COLLECTION; page 77 (left) MAURICE SEYMOUR/CLARKE-CRISP COLLECTION; page 77 (right) LIPNITZKI-VIOLLET; page 79 THEATRE MUSEUM/VICTORIA & ALBERT MUSEUM; page 80 BBC HULTON PICTURE LIBRARY; page 83 CLARKE-CRISP COLLECTION; page 84 GILBERT ADAMS; page 86 COLLECTION VIOLLET; page 88 (left) CLARKE-CRISP COLLECTION; page 88 (right) THEATRE MUSEUM/VICTORIA & ALBERT MUSEUM; page 90 SOCIETY FOR CULTURAL RELATIONS WITH THE USSR; page 91 ANDREW COCKRILL; page 93 SOCIETY FOR CULTURAL RELATIONS WITH THE USSR; page 95 CLARKE-CRISP COLLECTION; page 96 NOVOSTI PRESS AGENCY; page 97 ZOE DOMINIC/CLARKE-CRISP COLLECTION; page 98 (left & right) SOCIETY FOR CULTURAL RELATIONS WITH THE USSR; page 100 CLARKE-CRISP COLLECTION; page 101 DEE CONWAY; page 103 ANTHONY CRICKMAY/CLARKE-CRISP COLLECTION; page 104 ANDREW COCKRILL/CLARKE-CRISP COLLECTION; page 106 CLARKE-CRISP COLLECTION; page 109 (top) HOUSTON ROGERS/CLARKE CRISP COLLECTION; page 109 (bottom) CLARKE-CRISP COLLECTION; page 110 ROY ROUND/CLARKE-CRISP COLLECTION; page 110/111 CLARKE-CRISP COLLECTION; page 112 (left) SERGE LIDO; page 112 (right) DANIEL CANDE/CLARKE-CRISP COLLECTION; page 113 (left & right) RICHARD FARLEY/ BBC; page 114 KEITH MONEY/CLARKE-CRISP COLLECTION; page 117 KEITH MONEY; page 118 (left) EDWARD MANDINIAN III/ROYAL OPERA HOUSE; page 118 (right) DUNCAN MELVIN/ROYAL OPERA HOUSE;

page 119 CLARKE-CRISP COLLECTION; page 121 (top left) HOUSTON ROGERS/CLARKE-CRISP COLLECTION; page 121 (right) ANTHONY CRICKMAY/CLARKE-CRISP COLLECTION; page 121 (bottom left) BBC HULTON PICTURE LIBRARY; page 122 ANTHONY CRICKMAY/CLARKE-CRISP COLLECTION; page 123 (inset) CLARKE-CRISP COLLECTION; page 123 (main photo) ZOE DOMINIC/CLARKE-CRISP COLLECTION; page 124 (top left) ROY ROUND/CLARKE-CRISP COLLECTION; page 124 (top right) ANTHONY CRICKMAY; page 124 (bottom) CLARKE-CRISP COLLECTION; page 126 MARTHA SWOPE; page 129 CLARKE-CRISP COLLECTION; page 130 BBC HULTON PICTURE LIBRARY; page 131 FRED FEHL; page 133 (top & bottom) JOHN R. JOHNSEN; page 134 MARTHA SWOPE/CLARKE-CRISP COLLECTION; page 135 (top left & right) MARTHA SWOPE; page 135 (bottom) STEVEN CARAS/NYCB/CLARKE-CRISP COLLECTION; page 137 (top) LESLIE E. SPATT/CLARKE-CRISP COLLECTION; page 137 (bottom left & bottom right) FRED FEHL; page 138 (left) BBC HULTON PICTURE LIBRARY; page 138 (right) ANDREW COCKRILL; page 140 H. J. MYDTSKOV; page 142 H.J. MYDTSKOV; page 143 (top) CLARKE-CRISP COLLECTION; page 143 (bottom) ANTHONY CRICKMAY/CLARKE-CRISP COLLECTION; page 144/145 RIGMOR MYDTSKOV/DET KONGELIGE TEATER/CLARKE-CRISP COLLECTION; page 147 ZOE DOMINIC/LONDON FESTIVAL BALLET; page 150 CECIL BEATON/SOTHEBY'S, LONDON; page 152 MANSELL COLLECTION; page 153 THEATRE MUSEUM/VICTORIA & ALBERT MUSEUM; page 155 GILBERT ADAMS; page 156 ANTHONY CRICKMAY; page 159 CLARKE-CRISP COLLECTION; page 160 ANTHONY CRICKMAY/CLARKE-CRISP COLLECTION; page 161 JOHN R. JOHNSEN; page 162 MARTHA SWOPE; page 164 GORDON ANTHONY/THEATRE MUSEUM/VICTORIA & ALBERT MUSEUM; page 166/167 THEATRE MUSEUM/VICTORIA & ALBERT MUSEUM; page 168 JOHN R. JOHNSEN; page 169 MARTHA SWOPE; page 170 JØRGEN MYDTSKOV; page 171 CLARKE-CRISP COLLECTION; page 172 HOUSTON ROGERS/CLARKE-CRISP COLLECTION; page 173 (top) DINA MAKAROVA COLLECTION; page 173 (bottom) KEITH MONEY; page 176 ANTHONY CRICKMAY/CLARKE-CRISP COLLECTION; pages 177 & 178/179 THEATRE MUSEUM/VICTORIA & ALBERT MUSEUM; page 182 DINA MAKAROVA; page 183 HOUSTON ROGERS/THEATRE MUSEUM/VICTORIA & ALBERT MUSEUM; page 184 DEE CONWAY; page 185 (left) LESLIE E. SPATT; page 185 (right) KEITH MONEY; page 186 DEE CONWAY; page 187 THEATRE MUSEUM/VICTORIA & ALBERT MUSEUM; page 188 (left) NOVOSTI PRESS AGENCY; page 188 (right) LONDON FESTIVAL BALLET.

Index